151 Animals Stories

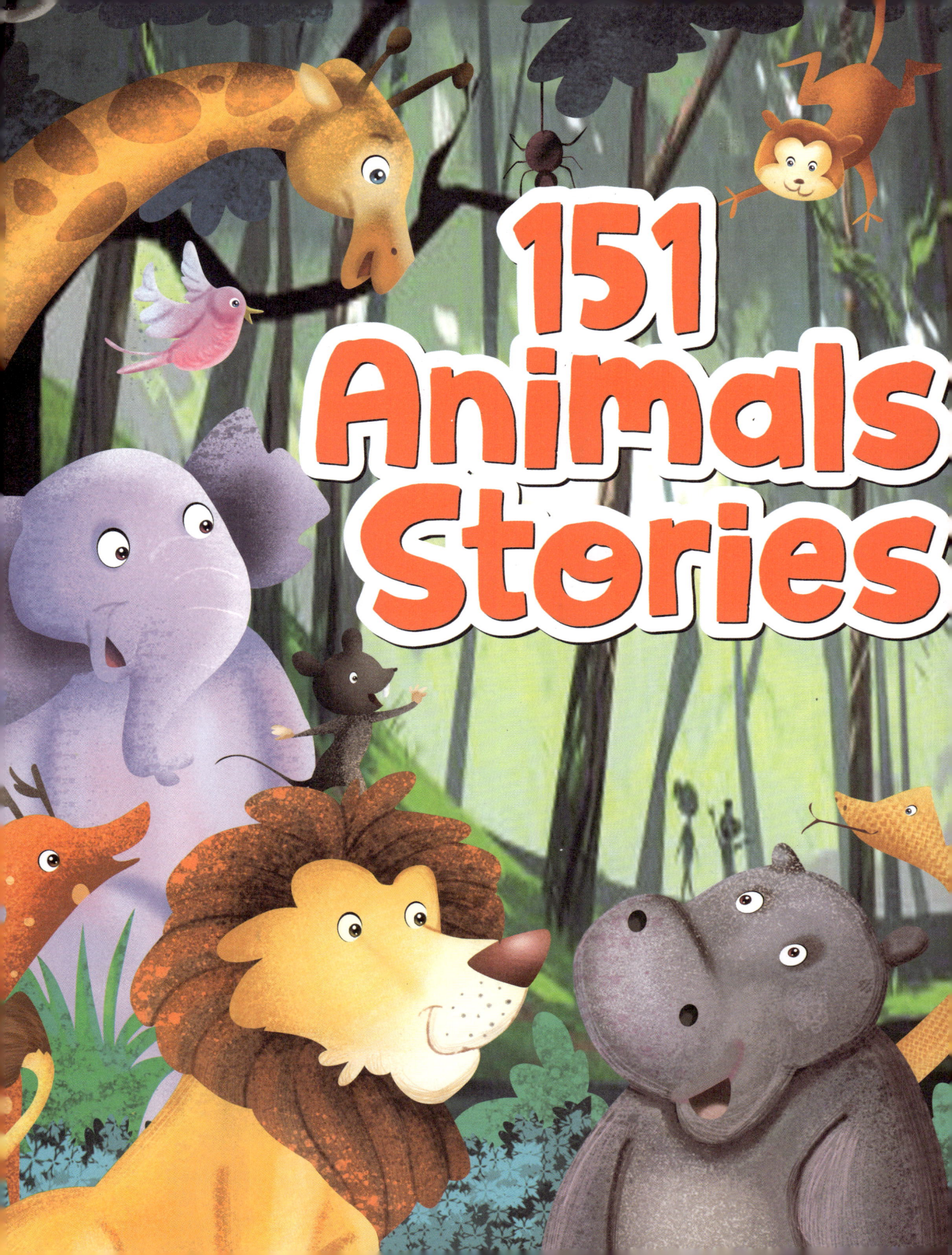

PEGASUS
www.pegasusforkids.com

© **B. Jain Publishers (P) Ltd.** All rights reserved. No part of this book may be reproduced, stored in a retrieval system or transmitted, in any form or by any means, mechanical, photocopying, recording or otherwise, without any prior written permission of the publisher.

Published by Kuldeep Jain for B. JAIN PUBLISHERS (P) Ltd., D-157, Sector 63, Noida - 201307, U.P
Registered office: 1921/10, Chuna Mandi, Paharganj, New Delhi-110055

Printed in India

Content

1. The Weasel and the Hens — 5
2. The Crows and the Serpent — 6
3. The Animal Olympics — 6
4. The Frog and the Serpent — 7
5. The Jackal and the Drum — 7
6. Teaching Sharks a Lesson — 8
7. The Littlest Elephant — 8
8. The Baby Koala on the Tree — 9
9. Eno and Beano — 9
10. The Cat, Partridge and the Hare — 10
11. The Cunning Hyena — 10
12. The Blue Jackal — 11
13. The Flea and the Mouse — 11
14. The Proud Rat — 12
15. The Perfect House — 12
16. The Toad and the Lamb — 13
17. The Generous Stag — 13
18. The Clever Minister — 14
19. The Bitter Enemies — 14
20. The Boastful Jackal — 15
21. Clever Timmy — 15
22. The Scared Lion — 16
23. The Cow in the Field — 16
24. I Want Sweets! — 17
25. The Blue Butterfly — 17
26. The Golden Firefly — 18
27. No One Loves Me! — 18
28. God Jupiter and the Turtle — 19
29. The Fight — 19
30. The Clever Fox Brothers — 20
31. Loving Molly — 20
32. Bumblebee's Lovely Garden — 21
33. Boe's Sword — 21
34. Bree's Nose — 22
35. The Tiger Brothers — 22
36. Bob and the Hyena — 23
37. The Little Brother — 23
38. The Crow and the Owl — 24
39. Ted, the Brave Bear — 24
40. The Playground — 25
41. A Good Deed — 25
42. The Mosquito Menace — 26
43. The Jackal and the Deer — 26
44. The Wolf and the Goat — 27
45. The Cunning Rabbit and the Coyote — 27
46. The Crow and the Raven — 28
47. The Magical Black Rose — 28
48. The Birthday Party — 29
49. The Old Zebra and his Tonic — 29
50. The Rabbit and the White Bird — 30
51. The Greedy Chipmunk — 30
52. The Queen's Armlet — 31
53. Rupert, the Red Nosed Reindeer — 31
54. The Wrong Message — 32
55. The Goat and the Giraffe — 32
56. How Crows Came Into Being — 33
57. The Elephant and the Mouse — 33
58. The Fire-Stick — 34
59. Toad and his Bruised Skin — 34
60. The Crows in the Corn — 35
61. The Lake of Pearl — 35
62. The Doe in the Box — 36
63. The Jealous Sisters — 36
64. The Best Bridegroom — 37
65. The Butterfly's Love for the Ant — 37
66. The Eagle and the Quail — 38
67. The Tiger and the Crane — 38
68. The Kangaroo and his Friends — 39
69. The Wicked Hermit — 39
70. The Monkeys and the Fish — 40
71. The Squirrel and the Tortoise — 40
72. Naughty Andrew — 41
73. The Foolish Monkey — 41
74. The Soft Red Ball — 42
75. The Magical Paint Brush — 42
76. The Most Beautiful Baby — 43
77. The Turkey and his Beard — 43
78. The Cheat Rice-Seller — 44

79. The Wolf and the Dancing Goat	44	
80. Lost and Found	45	
81. The Otter and the Bear	45	
82. The Drop of Honey	46	
83. The Simple Life	46	
84. The Blind Vulture	47	
85. The Father and the Son	47	
86. The Naughty Baby-Bear	48	
87. The Mongoose and the Snake	48	
88. Birds of a Flock	49	
89. Why Lizards Cannot Sit Upright	49	
90. Lazy Lizzie	50	
91. How the White Hen Got Speckles	50	
92. The Jackdaw and the Doves	51	
93. Water Turtles	51	
94. The Cotton Ghost	52	
95. The Daughter's Love	52	
96. The Hart and the Vine	53	
97. Hani, the Proud Peacock	53	
98. The Lame Donkey	54	
99. The Hawk and the Chickens	54	
100. Brave Sarah	55	
101. The Fox Meets his Match	55	
102. The Jealous Sparrow	56	
103. The Monkey Princess' Disguise	56	
104. The Swallows and the Snake	57	
105. The Unemployed Jackals	57	
106. The Clever Monkey	58	
107. The Two Parrots	58	
108. Panda Gummy	59	
109. The Hare and the Coyotes	59	
110. The Musical Jackal	60	
111. The Witty Old Owl	60	
112. Clever Suzy	61	
113. David's Mistake	61	
114. Hamy and the Oasis	62	
115. Abe and the Fish	62	
116. Sally Salmon	63	
117. The Parsley Queen	63	
118. The Greedy Lion	64	
119. The Camel, the Elephant and the Monkey	64	
120. The Gnat and the Lion	65	
121. Domi and his Cat	65	
122. The Lion and the Bull	66	
123. The Turkey With a Beautiful Heart	66	
124. The Elephant With Magical Powers	67	
125. The Penguin who was Scared of Snow	67	
126. Strange Friendship	68	
127. The Wolf-Stag	68	
128. The Vain Peacock	69	
129. The Elephant and his Blind Mother	69	
130. Movie Night	70	
131. The Kind and Hard Working Mouse	70	
132. The Best Soldier	71	
133. A Day With Daddy at Work	71	
134. Muss and Hector	72	
135. Wella, the Impatient Walrus	72	
136. The Kind Bear and the River God	73	
137. The Poor Cat and the Rich Cat	73	
138. The Great King of the Forest	74	
139. The Unfair Vixen	74	
140. The Hawk and the Bear	75	
141. The Poor Pigeon	75	
142. The Lion and the Fox	76	
143. The Sly Lion	76	
144. What Ringo Learnt	77	
145. The Heron, the Snake and the Mongoose	77	
146. White-Paw and the Kind Hawk	78	
147. The Elephant and the Giraffe	78	
148. Tina, the Kind Doe	79	
149. Elsie's Precious Jewels	79	
150. The Fox Cub	80	
151. The Lion and his Brothers	80	

The Weasel and the Hens

Once, some hens in a farm fell sick. A weasel living nearby came to know of this. He thought, 'This is my chance to grab the hens and make a meal of them!'
So, the cunning weasel disguised himself as a doctor and went to visit the hens.
He peeped inside the hens' coop and asked, 'How are you doing today?'
The clever hens were well aware of the weasel's pretences. They had recognised him in spite of his disguise. They rudely answered, 'We will be much better if you leave!'
The weasel realised that his trick had failed and left quietly.

The Crows and the Serpent

Two crows built a nest on a tree. But every time they laid eggs, a serpent would crawl up the tree and eat the eggs.

The crows were very sad so they went to a wise fox for help.

The fox said, 'Go to the palace and find something expensive. Throw it into the serpent's hole.'

The crows went to the palace and brought back the queen's necklace. They quickly threw it into the serpent's hole.

The palace guards had followed the crows. To get the necklace, they first killed the serpent. Thus, the crows got rid of the serpent!

The Animal Olympics

All the animals were excited about the 'Animal Olympics'.
Only the cheetah and tortoise were sad. The tortoise said, 'I am very slow. Even if I try hard, I can never win.'

The lion thought for a while and said, 'You can fire the pistol at the starting line.'

Then the cheetah said, 'I will certainly win, as I am the fastest animal. But then the others would have no fun in the contest.'

The lion said, 'You can carry the Olympic Torch.'

Thus, the cheetah and the tortoise took part in the Olympics even though they did not race.

The Frog and the Serpent

A frog once fought with the other frogs in a well. He angrily went to a serpent for help. He said, 'I want to punish the other frogs. Please eat them all. But you must spare my family.'
The serpent agreed. He ate up all the other frogs. Then he turned towards the frog's family.
The frog said, 'You promised to leave my family alone!'
The serpent laughed and said, 'You are a wicked frog. Why should I keep my promise to you?'
The frog realised his mistake. He quickly ran away with his family, and never tried to take revenge again.

The Jackal and the Drum

A hungry jackal was looking for food. He heard a loud noise and was very frightened by it. Looking around, he found a war drum lying nearby. The breeze was making a tree branch strike it again and again.
But the jackal did not know that it was just a drum! He thought, 'What a huge, strange animal. It must be delicious.'
Without wasting another moment, he sprang at the drum. His sharp nails pierced the drum, and tore it.
Now at last he realised that it was just a drum. Feeling foolish, he quietly ran away from there.

Teaching Sharks a Lesson

One day, baby whale was playing by himself when four sharks came over and teased him wickedly, 'Can we eat you? You look mighty tasty to us.'
The poor baby whale ran back to his house and hid under his bed. Terrified, he recounted the tale to his mother. The next day, baby whale was again playing by himself when the same sharks came and teased him.
Suddenly, four big whales came out of the weeds and said, 'Hey sharks! Can we eat you? You look mighty tasty to us!'
The sharks swam away scared and never troubled baby whale again.

The Littlest Elephant

One day, a herd of elephants was crossing a river carefully as the river was flooded. 'Tan-tan-taraaa!' Suddenly, the head elephant trumpeted loudly to let his herd know that there was danger.
Now, the littlest elephant was just a few weeks old, and had never swum in such strong flood. He was scared for a moment, but then he heard his mother's trumpet. Immediately, he started swimming towards the sound.
He did not give up, and finally managed to cross over safely. All the older elephants praised him and trumpeted loudly to celebrate the little elephant's triumph.

The Baby Koala on the Tree

Once, baby koala was learning how to climb trees. 'This is fun!' he thought.

Soon becoming tired, he climbed the tallest tree and went to sleep. His parents did not want to wake him up and left. After a while, the Baby Koala woke up. He found that his parents were not there.

'Oh no! How will I come down now?' he thought as he couldn't climb down without help.

Suddenly, an old hyena, with one eye, came and asked slyly, 'Can I help you down?'

But little koala politely said, 'No, thank you.' He knew the hyena would eat him up. Just then, a huge group of koala bears came with sticks and stones in their hands. The hyena saw them and ran away.

Then, baby koala's father came, took him down from the branch and back home.

Eno and Beano

Eno and Beano were two squirrels. Everyday, they collected nuts. They ate a few, and stored the rest for winter.

One day, Eno saw that some nuts were missing from the pile. He thought, 'Maybe Beano ate them.' When Beano noticed the missing nuts, he called out, 'Why have you eaten all those nuts, Eno?' Eno said, 'I thought you had eaten them!' Suddenly, they saw a nut roll down from the pile. It rolled straight out of the house! The two squirrels started laughing. They made a box to put the nuts in, and no more nuts rolled away!

The Cat, Partridge and the Hare

A partridge lived under a tree. One day, when she went to find food, a hare entered her house. He liked it so much that he started living there.

When the partridge came home, she was upset and said, 'This is my house. You cannot live here.'

The hare said, 'Let us ask the wise cat what we should do.'

They went to the cat and told him everything. But the cat was only pretending to be wise. He waited until they came close enough, and ate both of them!

Since that day, hares and partridges do not trust cats.

The Cunning Hyena

Once, a cunning hyena decided to trick a monkey. He said, 'I bet I know more tricks than you.'

The monkey replied, 'I only know one trick—how to escape from danger.'

The cunning hyena said, 'If my trick to escape danger is better, you must give me food for a week.'

Suddenly, the monkey heard the howling of hunting dogs. He said, 'Forget the food! If you don't hide at once, the dogs will catch you. Then no trick can save you!'

The monkey climbed the tree, while the hyena ran away as fast as he could!

The Blue Jackal

A jackal was once running from some wild dogs. He ran and ran, till he fell into a tub of indigo dye. This made him blue in colour! All the animals thought he was a new, powerful animal. The clever jackal told them, 'The gods have sent me to rule this forest.'
So the animals made him king and took good care of him.
But one day, a pack of jackals passed by. The blue jackal howled out to them out of habit. The animals realised that he was just a normal jackal, and drove him out of the forest.

The Flea and the Mouse

One day, a flea bit a lion. The lion called some jackals to kill the flea.
The flea was scared. He saw that a little mouse lived nearby. The flea begged the mouse, 'Please let me hide here.'
The mouse agreed. The flea said, 'I will repay your kindness one day.'
A few days later, a jackal caught the mouse. Just when the jackal was about to eat it, the flea bit the jackal on the hand. The jackal cried out and let the mouse go. The mouse hurried back to its hole.
Thus, the flea repaid the mouse.

The Proud Rat

One day, a rat was running around a beetle, just to show off how fast he was.
'Have you seen my speed, you simple beetle?' cried the proud rat.
A parrot was watching the rat. He called out, 'Let's see you race. The winner will get a bright, colourful new coat.'
The race started. The rat was surprised to see the beetle flying past, instead of running. The beetle reached the finishing line much before the proud rat.
The parrot gave the beetle a green and gold coat, and told the rat, 'Remember, never judge anyone by his looks alone.'

The Perfect House

Once, the stag and tiger both wanted to build houses. The stag found the perfect place and cleared half the area. Later, the tiger also liked the same place and cleared the remaining area.
Next morning, the stag laid the foundation for the house. That night, the tiger built the walls. The next day, the stag made a roof of dry grass. He went inside and fell asleep.
The tiger came there at night. Both the animals were so scared to see someone else there, that they both ran in different directions! Thus, they both left the perfect house empty!

The Toad and the Lamb

A lamb was very proud of himself. One day, a toad said, 'You should not be so proud. I am so small, yet I am faster than you.'
The lamb said, 'I will believe that if you can defeat me in a race.'
The toad agreed. On the day of the race, the toad's relatives hid all along the racetrack, and started running as soon as they saw the lamb. Thus, whenever the lamb looked up, he saw a toad in front of him! At the finish line, too, the Toad was already waiting.
The lamb was never proud again.

The Generous Stag

There once lived a very generous stag in a forest. One day, he met a poor python begging for food and shelter.
The kind stag let python stay in his house. The stag's friends said, 'The python cannot be trusted. He is dangerous.'
But the stag ignored them all. After a month, the python went away without informing the stag.
'I am not upset, because it was my decision to shelter him,' said the stag. 'I did not expect him to thank me, so I do not feel bad.'
The stag's friends realised this was true, and stopped scolding him.

The Clever Minister

Once, a lion king faced a strange case. A bear merchant said, 'Majesty, this elephant promised to pay 'nothing' more than the price of goods. He has paid for the goods but didn't give me 'nothing'.'

The elephant said, 'But 'nothing' is nothing.'

The minister fox, hearing their quarrel had an idea and he brought a bowl of water before them. He said, 'Bear, dip your fist in the water. Then, take your fist out and open it.'

The bear did this. The fox asked, 'What is in your fist?'

The bear replied, 'Nothing!'

The fox said, 'Now, you have 'nothing' in your fist.' The bear understood his mistake and lion rewarded the clever fox.

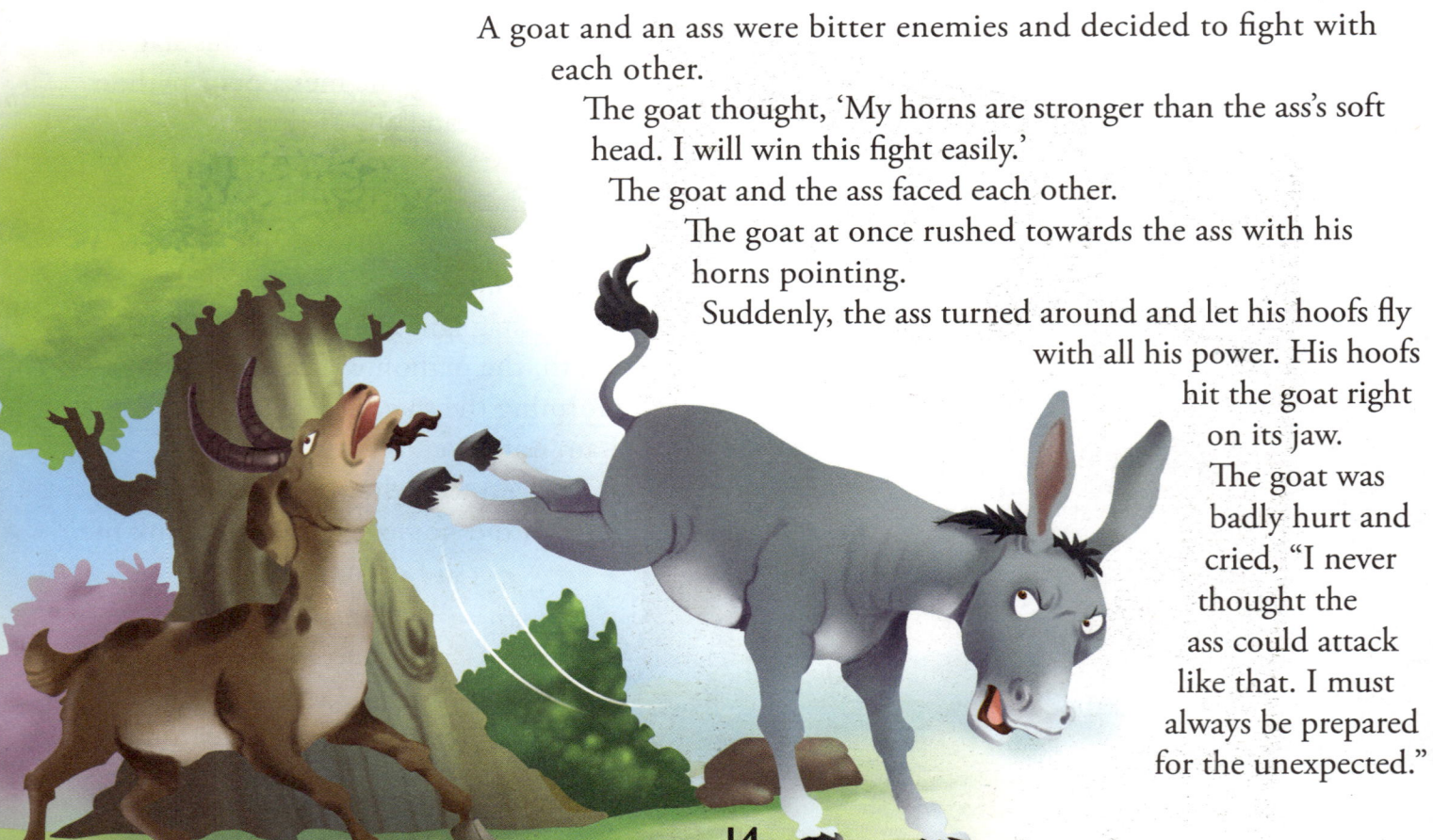

The Bitter Enemies

A goat and an ass were bitter enemies and decided to fight with each other.

The goat thought, 'My horns are stronger than the ass's soft head. I will win this fight easily.'

The goat and the ass faced each other.

The goat at once rushed towards the ass with his horns pointing.

Suddenly, the ass turned around and let his hoofs fly with all his power. His hoofs hit the goat right on its jaw.

The goat was badly hurt and cried, "I never thought the ass could attack like that. I must always be prepared for the unexpected."

The Boastful Jackal

A jackal wanted to be the king of the jungle. One day, he looked at the ground and saw his long shadow. The jackal thought, 'I am so tall and huge! Indeed, I am mightier than the lion. I should certainly become the king.'
Thus, the jackal set out for the lion's den and shouted, 'Lion! Even my shadow is mightier than you are. Therefore, I will be the king from now on.'
The lion laughed at the jackal and said, 'If it is really so mighty, then your shadow should be the king, and not you.'
Saying this, the lion pounced on the foolish jackal. The jackal ran as fast as he could. He never behaved so foolishly again!

Clever Timmy

Timmy tortoise was going to visit his grandmother. On the way, he met a jackal, who said, 'I will eat you up.'
Clever Timmy said, 'I'm going to my granny's place. I will come back fatter than before. Then you can have a good meal out of me.'
The jackal agreed. At grandmother's house, Timmy ate a lot of delicious food. While returning home, Timmy thought of a plan to fool the jackal. So he dressed himself in strange rags and painted his face red.
When the jackal saw him, he did not recognise Timmy at all! In fact, he kept wondering who the strange animal was. Thus clever Timmy confused the jackal and reached home safely.

The Scared Lion

Once, there was a lion who was very scared of everything—water, wind, rain, other animals, even smaller creatures like mice and worms.
'Behave like a lion!' his friends advised him. But he did not know how! He hated terrifying and eating smaller animals, like his family members did.
Then, a wise old cheetah told him, 'If you don't want to scare others, then don't! At least stop being afraid of everything. You can be a friend and counsellor to others.'
From then on, the lion became a friend to other animals and ate vegetables and fruits with them. He was finally happy.

The Cow in the Field

Once, Sally, the cow, was walking through a field. Just then, she saw Tom, the dog. Sally asked, 'Tom, have you seen my calf?'
Tom exclaimed, 'Yes, I saw him at the edge of the forest.'
Sally was worried, she said, 'Thank you, Tom, I'll go and bring him back.'
Tom also went with Sally.
As they reached the edge of the forest, they saw a wolf about to pounce on the calf.
Tom started barking loudly. The wolf saw them and ran away. Sally thanked Tom for saving her calf. Then, she took her calf back to their home in the field.

I Want Sweets!

Mia, the camel, loved eating sweets. 'I don't want food. It is boring. All those fruits and vegetables, ughh!' she snorted in disgust.
'Try eating them, Mia. They taste really good,' said her friend. But after eating sweets, Mia had no appetite left for anything else. One morning, Mia got up with a severe tooth-ache. She went to the dentist. 'What have you been eating?' the dentist exclaimed. Mia had to tell him. Hearing this, the dentist told her that two of her teeth had cavities in them. He then took out two of Mia's teeth and cleaned the rest. He made her promise to eat fewer sweets and candies and more fruits and vegetables. Slowly, her teeth became much better!

The Blue Butterfly

Once, a little butterfly came out of its cocoon. Its wings were a beautiful blue. In the sunshine, the colours of its wings gleamed like jewels! But the butterfly did not know it was beautiful. It was scared. How would it use these large wings? What if they stopped working and it fell? Just then, the butterfly caught the wonderful scent of nectar. It forgot all about its worries and acted on instinct.
It flew up in the air and landed on the delicate petals of a flower. The blue butterfly drank the delicious nectar, and was never scared again!

The Golden Firefly

A poor cat was looking for something to eat in the garbage dump when he found a wooden box. When he opened it, a golden firefly came out of it and said, 'You have freed me. A wicked magician had tricked and trapped me inside it. Since you have saved me, I shall grant you a wish.' The cat wondered, 'Should I ask for money or should I ask for food?' Then finally, he said, 'As I have only one wish, here it is. I want you to fix all my problems.'
Thus, the firefly solved all his problems and vanished. The cat was happy.

No One Loves Me!

One day, angry with his parents, a baby elephant left home.
Meanwhile, the baby elephant's mother had made banana-pudding for him. She sent a little birdie to bring him home.
However, baby elephant refused to go home. 'No one loves me!' he cried.
The birdie said, 'Our parents scold us for our own good. Your parents love you a lot and that's why your mother baked a banana pudding just for you.'
Baby elephant ran all the way home. Indeed, his mother had a bowl of banana-pudding ready for him! He took it from her and promised never to leave home again.

God Jupiter and the Turtle

A long time ago, God Jupiter was celebrating his wedding and invited all the animals on earth for the celebrations. Everyone was present, except the turtle. Jupiter was curious to know why the turtle was missing. So he called him specially and asked him, 'Turtle, why among all the animals, did you not come?'

The turtle calmly replied, 'Why would I have made the long journey? I enjoyed sitting in my house!'

Jupiter was so angry at his lazy answer that he punished the turtle to take his house on his back, forever.

To this day, turtles live in their shells.

The Fight

Baby rhino and baby hippo were best friends. They loved playing together and running behind butterflies.

Once, while coming back from school, baby hippo said, 'When baby deer called me fat, you also laughed. That was mean!'

Baby rhino replied, 'I was not laughing! Now you are not being nice.'

Both of them stomped off home in anger.

The next morning, baby rhino went to baby hippo's house and said, 'I am sorry to have hurt you. You are not fat at all. I am proud to be your best friend.'

Baby hippo hugged his friend and the fight was forgotten.

The Clever Fox Brothers

One day, two fox brothers had captured a quail. They were so happy that they started celebrating.

Hearing all the noise they were making, a wolf came there. Seeing the dead quail on the ground, he grabbed it and said, 'This will make me a delicious dinner.'

The brothers decided to take help from their friends, the hyenas, to get back the quail. They promised the hyenas a share of the quail.

The hyenas agreed to help them and drove the wolf away. But as soon as the wolf dropped the quail, the fox brothers took it and ran inside a little hole. There they ate the quail before the hyenas returned.

When the hyenas realised what had happened, they tried to reach the foxes, but the hole was too small for them. They went away in disgust and said, 'It is our fault for trusting false friends.'

Loving Molly

Once, a strange sickness affected all the children of the forest. Molly, the elephant, knew a lot about herbal remedies, so she mixed some herbs and fed this medicine to all the sick children.

She stayed with them and looked after them day and night. The children soon became well again.

Sadly, since she did not eat or sleep at all, Molly fell seriously ill. Because no one else knew how to make medicines, Molly died soon after. The children were sad and cried at her burial. They said, 'We are grateful that you saved our lives.' They decided to learn how to make medicines and never let anyone else die because of illness. Thus, Molly's sacrifice was never forgotten.

Bumblebee's Lovely Garden

Little bumblebee loved honey. One year, in spring, he worked hard at planting his own garden.
'I will plant sunflowers, wild-lilac, chrysanthemum and rosemary in my garden. They are beautiful and their nectar is equally sweet,' thought the bumblebee.
He sowed the seeds and watered them everyday. He cleaned his flower-beds regularly. Every morning, the first thing he checked was if his flowers were blooming.
One morning, 'Look! Mum and dad,' screamed bumblebee, 'the flowers are blooming big and bright.'
'We are so proud of you, dear son,' said mum to a beaming bumblebee. Bumblebee's hard work had paid off as he now had a beautiful garden.

Boe's Sword

Once, there lived a brave warrior bear named Boe. He was soon going to marry a beautiful bear named Fiona. But a monkey named Gunthy also loved Fiona.
One day, Gunthy snuck into Boe's house and stole Boe's sword. He left behind a note that said, 'The sword will be returned if Fiona marries Gunthy.'
Boe dressed up as Fiona and went to Gunthy's house. He spoke in a sweet voice, 'May I have a look at your sword?'
Foolish Gunthy thought it was really Fiona! He started showing it off and handed it to Boe. As soon as he got the sword in his hands, brave Boe defeated Gunthy and returned home victorious.

Bree's Nose

Once, a naughty reindeer, Bree was playing in a glade with his friends. Suddenly, a zebra came running. 'Everyone run home, at once! A bear broke a beehive with a stone. All the bees are now flying towards our play-glade.'
Everyone ran home, except Bree. She kept playing.
Suddenly, a buzz of bees flew into the glade and stung Bree on the nose.
Bree cried out in pain and ran home. Bree's mother took her to doctor rabbit. He applied some medicine on her nose.
In two days, Bree's nose finally healed and she promised always to listen to others!

The Tiger Brothers

Once, two tiger brothers had split the forest into two kingdoms. However, the younger brother thought his elder brother had cheated him. So, the brothers neither met nor spoke to each other.
One night, the elder brother dreamt of his mother, who said, 'You have to reach out to your brother.'
The next day, he sent his minister, the fox, to his younger brother. The fox said, 'Your Majesty, your brother remembers you fondly and wishes to see you.'
Now, the younger brother also missed his brother and wanted to make peace with him. He rushed to meet his brother. How delighted they were to see each other! After that day, they lived happily together.

Bob and the Hyena

Bob, the deer, lived with his family. Once, a wicked hyena walked into his house and started living there. He ate everything in the house and snored loudly at night!
Finally, Bob decided to get rid of him. He challenged the hyena to a porridge eating competition, saying, 'If you manage to eat your share first, you shall win. But if you lose, you must leave our house.'
The hyena thought that he would win easily and agreed. As they both started eating, Bob secretly poured his porridge into a pouch hidden under his shirt. Thus, he managed to finish his bowl first!
The hyena lost the competition and left the house.

The Little Brother

Once, a little giraffe pleaded with his parents, 'Please, can you bring a brother for me?' His father replied, 'We will do that, if you promise to be good and listen to your elders. Mommy will go to the hospital and she will bring your brother from there.'
So, from that day, little giraffe helped mommy and daddy at home and completed his homework on time as well.
Finally, one night mommy went to the hospital.
The next morning, little giraffe jumped with joy to see that he had a cute little brother. Little giraffe was no longer little; he was a big brother now!

The Crow and the Owl

Once, an intelligent crow met a wise owl. The crow said to the owl, 'I have heard that you are the wisest teacher. Please share your wisdom about the universe with me.'

The wise owl knew that the crow was intelligent. But he also knew that the crow did not share what he knew with others. So he invited the crow to sit down. Then he picked up a big pot and began pouring out some tea. The cup was soon full; however he continued to pour. Soon, the cup started overflowing.

The owl said, 'You are like this cup, full of knowledge. You must put it to use or else it will be wasted, just like this tea.'

The crow understood what the owl was trying to tell him. He thanked him and started teaching others.

Ted, the Brave Bear

Once, six bears set out to find brides for themselves. Ted, their seventh brother, however, stayed back at home. Some time passed and the brothers were returning home. However, on their way back, they were captured by a tiger.

Ted learnt about this and reached the tiger's den. There, he met a beautiful bear whom the tiger had also captured.

Ted was brave. He attacked the tiger and fought him for many hours. Finally, the tiger gave up. Ted thus saved his brothers, their wives and the beautiful bear. Ted married the beautiful bear and they all lived very happily for many years.

The Playground

Anna, the monkey was sad. She had recently come to a live in a new forest and did not know anyone there. She went to the playground and slid down the slide. Immediately Peter, the panda came sliding down behind her.
'Do you know how to slide up? It's fun,' he said. He climbed up and Anna followed. Peter slipped and both fell in a pile of mud, laughing loudly. Hearing the laughter, the alligator also joined in, followed by the elephant, bear and deer. Soon, everyone fell in a pile.
'This is fun!' said Anna laughingly.
Anna left the playground grinning, 'It is so much fun making new friends! Anna was no longer sad.'

A Good Deed

Tessy was a very kind and helpful chipmunk. One day, she helped an old hare by carrying the hare's heavy bag. The hare rewarded Tessy with a magical box, which was always full of nuts. Rosy, Tessy's elder sister was jealous when she heard about this. She was very different from Tessy and was selfish and rude. Now she, also went to the market. But when the hare asked for help, Rosy refused.

The old hare decided to punish her and said, 'You won't be able to eat anything unless you help at least one person every day.'
From that day onwards, Rosy could not eat even the tiniest nut unless she helped someone first! Over time, she began to like helping people, and became a much nicer person.

The Mosquito Menace

The weather was warm after the long chilly winters. All the animals rejoiced with the coming of summer. 'That grass looks lovely,' thought the bear. Suddenly he was surrounded by mosquitoes, which bit him all over. 'I will catch some fish,' thought the eagle. But soon he too was covered in mosquito bites. The animals did not know what to do. So they all went to the wise owl. The wise owl said, 'Nature has all the answers to your questions. As soon as summer is over, the mosquitoes will disappear on their own!' Sure enough, with the first cool breeze, the animals breathed a sigh of relief. The mosquitoes were finally gone! All the animals thanked the wise owl for his advice.

The Jackal and the Deer

A deer became friends with a clever jackal. One day, they went to a corn field. They were eating the corn, when the deer's foot got caught in a hidden trap!

The wicked jackal said, 'I tricked you so easily! Now the humans will kill you. Then I will eat you up.'

Luckily, some friendly birds saw what happened. They flew down and told the deer what to do. So accordingly, the deer lay down and pretended to be dead. Later, as soon as the farmer opened the trap, the deer ran away while the jackal got beaten up the farmer. The deer thanked the birds and never trusted the jackal again.

The Wolf and the Goat

A hungry wolf saw a goat eating grass on top of a high cliff. He thought, 'I wish this goat would climb down from the cliff, so I could eat it!'

He thought of a plan and said, 'Dear friend, is it not dangerous for you to be at such a great height? Please come down before you hurt yourself.'

The goat was also clever. He said, 'You do not care if I hurt myself or not. What you really care about is eating me.'

The wolf understood that the goat would not be fooled. So, he quietly went away.

The Cunning Rabbit and the Coyote

Once, a coyote saw a rabbit holding a big rock upright.

He asked, 'Why you are holding up this rock. Maybe I could help you?'

Rabbit said, 'I am holding this rock so that the sky will not crash on my head.'

The coyote thought, 'The rabbit is so weak. If he lets the rock fall, the sky will fall too!'

So, he requested the rabbit to let him hold the rock instead. The rabbit agreed.

Hours later, the coyote was so tired that he let the rock fall. He had realised by now that the sky had not fallen, but the rabbit had surely fooled him!

The Crow and the Raven

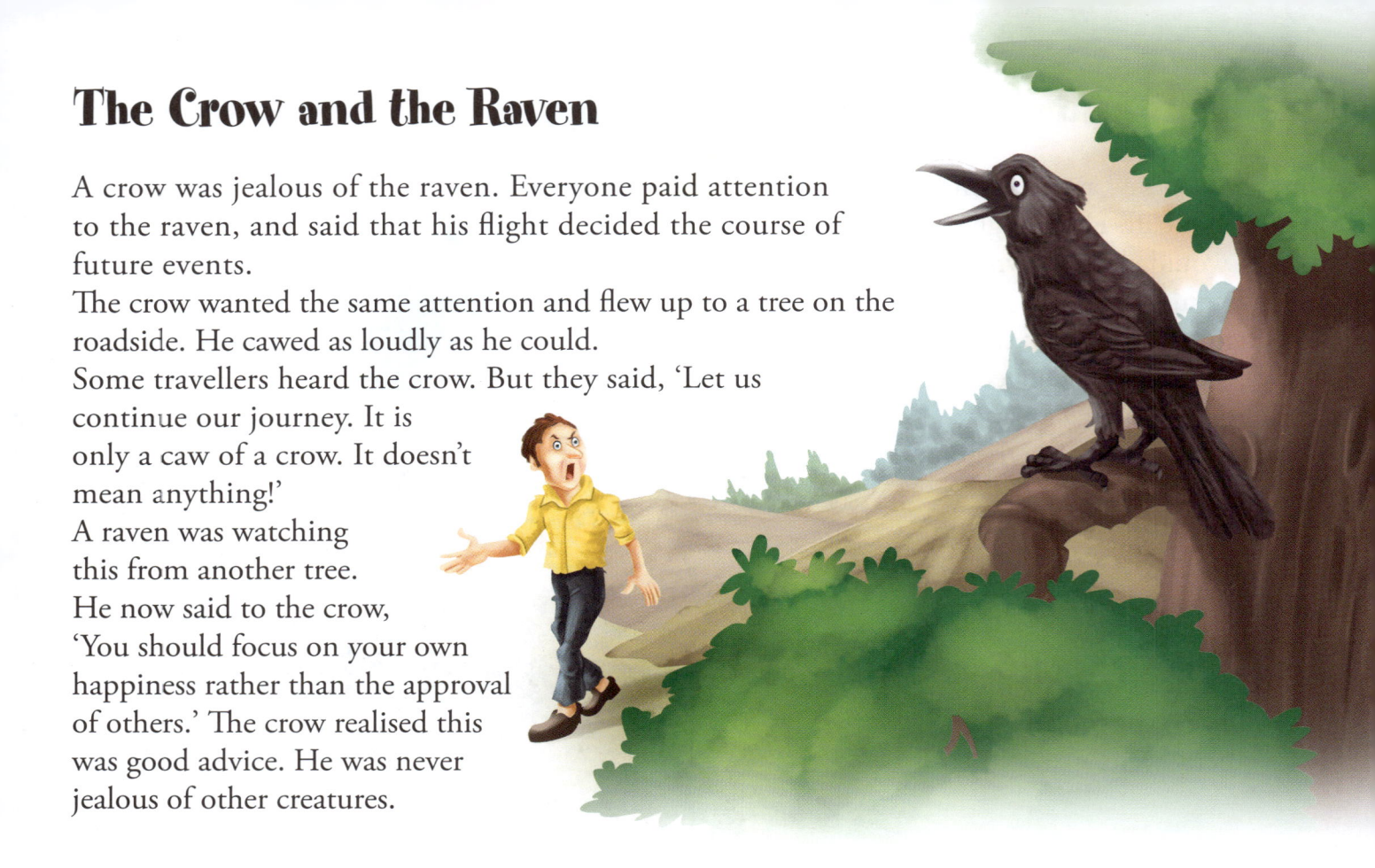

A crow was jealous of the raven. Everyone paid attention to the raven, and said that his flight decided the course of future events.

The crow wanted the same attention and flew up to a tree on the roadside. He cawed as loudly as he could.

Some travellers heard the crow. But they said, 'Let us continue our journey. It is only a caw of a crow. It doesn't mean anything!'

A raven was watching this from another tree. He now said to the crow, 'You should focus on your own happiness rather than the approval of others.' The crow realised this was good advice. He was never jealous of other creatures.

The Magical Black Rose

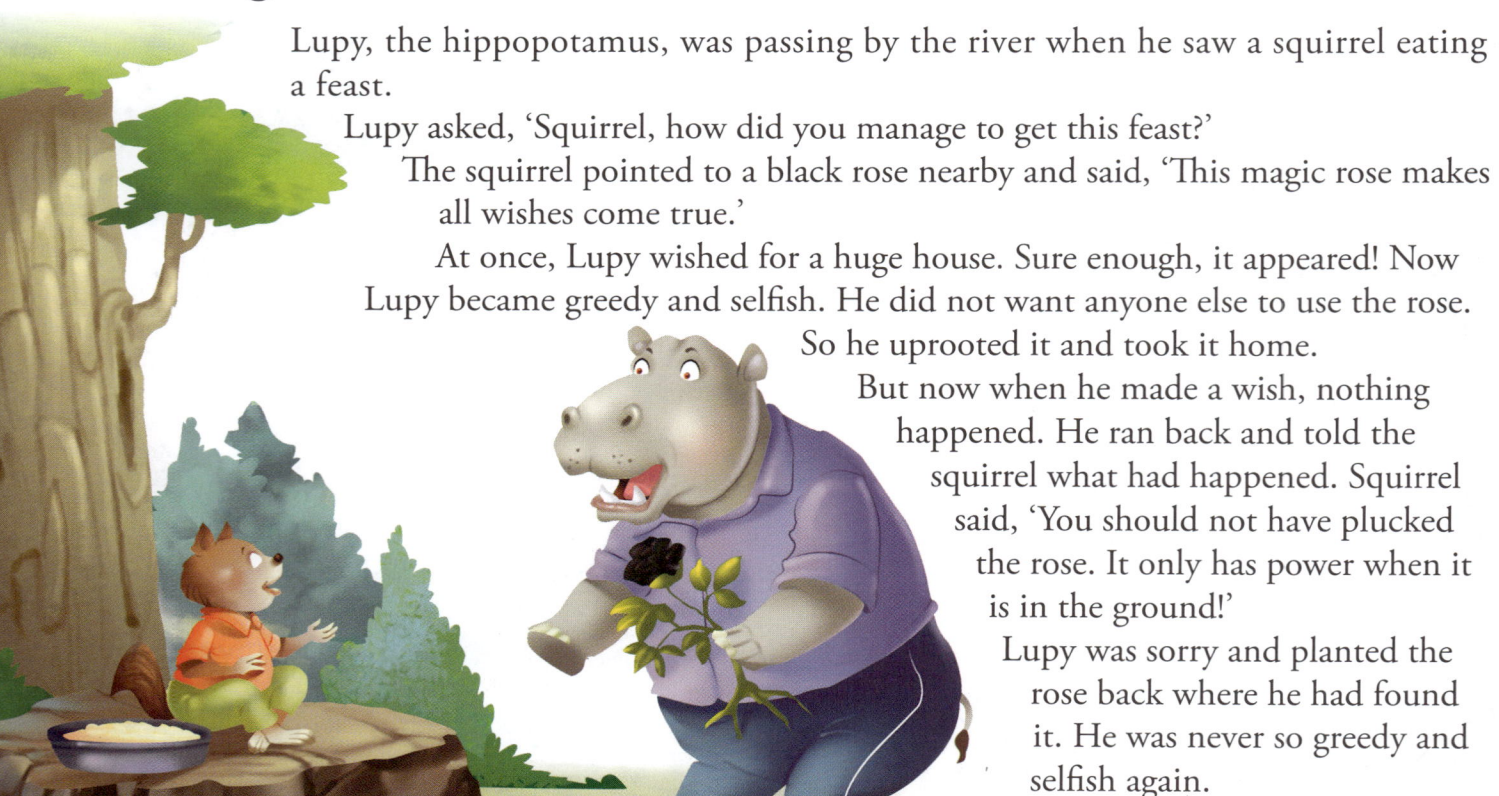

Lupy, the hippopotamus, was passing by the river when he saw a squirrel eating a feast.

Lupy asked, 'Squirrel, how did you manage to get this feast?'

The squirrel pointed to a black rose nearby and said, 'This magic rose makes all wishes come true.'

At once, Lupy wished for a huge house. Sure enough, it appeared! Now Lupy became greedy and selfish. He did not want anyone else to use the rose. So he uprooted it and took it home.

But now when he made a wish, nothing happened. He ran back and told the squirrel what had happened. Squirrel said, 'You should not have plucked the rose. It only has power when it is in the ground!'

Lupy was sorry and planted the rose back where he had found it. He was never so greedy and selfish again.

The Birthday Party

'Cut the cake! Cut the cake!' chanted Patricia's friends. But the little monkey was sad. Papa had not come back from work yet.

Mother said, 'Papa might get late, let's cut the cake in the meantime.' Suddenly, with a loud ringing of bells, a huge orangutan came in and started singing, 'Happy birthday!' for Patricia. Excited, she also joined in and cut the cake. They all played fun games after that. A little while later, the orangutan hugged Patricia and whispered 'Happy birthday' in her papa's voice! It was her papa dressed up as an orangutan to make Patricia's party exciting!

The Old Zebra and his Tonic

A zebra herd was about to migrate for the winter. But an old zebra decided that he was too old to move.

Everybody was sad to leave him, but the old zebra said, 'Please, go ahead without me!

One young zebra had an idea. He collected some green leaves and dried them in the sun. He ground the leaves, adding water to them. Then he gave this mixture to the old zebra, saying, 'This tonic will make you feel much better.'

The old zebra drank up the tonic and immediately felt very energetic. He was able to make the journey along with the herd without any problems. Finally he asked the young zebra, 'What did you put in that excellent tonic?'

The young zebra smiled and said, 'It was just a mixture of dried leaves. But it gave you the confidence to travel so far. That is why I tricked you.'

The old zebra laughed and thanked the young zebra for his thoughtfulness.

The Rabbit and the White Bird

Once, there lived three rabbit sisters. One day, the eldest sister lost her fur coat in the meadow.
While searching, she met a white bird who said, 'I will help you if you will marry me.' She refused.
The same thing happened to the second sister, who also refused to marry the bird. But when the youngest sister met the bird, she agreed to marry him.
They were married, and the next morning, a handsome rabbit brought the missing fur coat home!
'I am that white bird,' he said. 'By marrying me, you have broken the spell that had made me a bird. Thank you!'
From that day, they lived happily together.

The Greedy Chipmunk

A greedy chipmunk loved eating eggs. There was not a single nest which he had not broken or from where he had not stolen eggs.

His neighbour, the mouse, warned him, 'You have to stop. Your stealing habits will get you into trouble.' But the chipmunk merrily continued to steal.

One day, a mouse saw the chipmunk with a big egg, rubbing his hands in glee. He warned, 'This seems like an owl's egg. Put it back!'

But before the chipmink could do anything, an angry owl swooped down on him. Within minutes, the chipmunk was dead due to his greed.

The Queen's Armlet

A lioness queen was bathing in the river. Her maids placed her clothes and jewellery in a neat pile under a tree.
A monkey, sitting on the same tree, rushed down and grabbed the queen's armlet.
'Oh no!' cried the maids, 'The monkey has taken the armlet!'
Just then, a young bear came with a bunch of bananas and started peeling them. The greedy monkey rushed down to grab a few bananas before the bear ate them all up, leaving behind the armlet. The maids quickly got back the armlet. The queen was happy and she rewarded the bear handsomely who had helped her unknowingly.

Rupert, the Red Nosed Reindeer

Rupert had a red nose. So, his school-mates teased him and called him, 'Red nose candy.' But they didn't know that his smelling power was sharper than the other reindeers.

Once, during recess at school, when everyone was playing together, Rupert sat alone. Suddenly, he smelt danger for a lion was nearby! Rupert screamed loudly, 'Run everyone, get inside. There is danger close by.' Everyone did as he said. Five minutes later, they peeped from the school windows and saw a disappointed lion that had been planning to eat the reindeers. Everyone thanked Rupert and never made fun of the nose that had saved them.

The Wrong Message

It is believed that the Creator once said to his messenger, the donkey, 'Let every animal on earth know that they should be kind and loving to everyone else, as they are brothers and sisters!'
Halfway to the earth, the donkey began eating grass. Then he suddenly remembered his task but forgot what the message was. So the donkey said, 'The Creator has said that brothers and sisters should be kind to each other.'
Hearing this, everyone started behaving nicely only towards their own siblings, but not towards others. The Creator was upset when he saw this.
He punished the donkey, 'From now on you cannot talk, you will just bray!' The donkey was sorry for his forgetfulness.

The Goat and the Giraffe

A goat and a giraffe were very good friends. The goat often said, 'You are so tall that you look awkward!' But the giraffe remained silent. Once, the summer was very harsh and all the grass and small plants started drying. 'Oh I wish it would rain!' the goat cried. But it did not rain and the goat was hungry for days.
Soon, only the tree-tops were left with a few leaves which were beyond the goat's reach. One day, the kind giraffe plucked them and said, 'You eat these, dear friend. I'm not hungry. I will eat later.'
The goat felt ashamed and said, 'I used to tease you but now it is your height that has helped me. I am very sorry for making fun of you!' The giraffe forgave him.

How Crows Came Into Being

Long ago, a frog loved listening to a cuckoo's song. 'You sing beautifully,' croaked the frog. She was pleased and agreed to teach him how to sing.
'La, la, la,' the cuckoo sang melodiously.
'La, la, la,' the frog croaked, trying hard to soften his harsh voice.
As the weeks passed, the cuckoo had to hear him croaking all day, and even dreamt of the croaking at night.
Then one day, the cuckoo tried to sing, but the only sound that came out was 'Caww... cawwww!' She could not sing! And that is how crows came into being!

The Elephant and the Mouse

Toby was a vain elephant. 'I am stronger than everyone else. Even lions are scared of me,' he thought.

His parents always told him, 'Toby, don't think like that. Sometimes even the smallest animal can become the strongest.' But Toby did not believe them.

Once while playing he fell in a fox's trap. He tried really hard but could not free himself. But Will, the mouse, saw Toby in danger and immediately came and freed him. Toby was very thankful. He realised that even though Will was small, he saved Toby from a terrible fate. Toby was never vain again.

The Fire-Stick

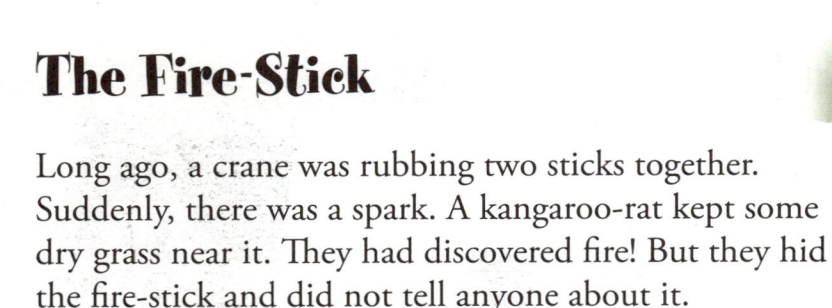

Long ago, a crane was rubbing two sticks together. Suddenly, there was a spark. A kangaroo-rat kept some dry grass near it. They had discovered fire! But they hid the fire-stick and did not tell anyone about it.

One day, a parrot found out their secret. He thought that fire should be shared. So he held a huge carnival and invited all the animals.

There were so many exciting things at the carnival that the crane and the kangaroo-rat forgot about the fire-stick.

The parrot, meanwhile, stole the fire-stick and told everyone how to use it. Since that day, fire was no longer a secret between the crane and the kangaroo-rat!

Toad and his Bruised Skin

Long ago, the toad had smooth skin. Then one day, all the animals, except the toad, were invited to a party in the sky.

The toad was a little upset, but he made a clever plan to attend the party. He said to a buzzard, 'Take your violin along, for you are a brilliant musician.'

The buzzard thought this was a good idea. On the day of the party, the toad slipped into the buzzard's violin. But when the buzzard was carrying the violin to the party, he accidentally dropped it!

The poor toad got badly hurt. From that day, he has bruises all over his skin!

The Crows in the Corn

Once, a deer and his wife were sleeping late on a Sunday morning. Some naughty crows that lived in the trees near their farm cawed in excitement, 'Let us eat the ripe corn in the field.' So, they all started to eat the corn. Seeing them, an old rooster cried, 'The crows are in the corn! The crows are in the corn!' The deer and his wife heard the rooster's cry but they did not wake up. When they finally woke up, all the corn was gone and so were the crows! They repented for not waking up when the rooster had alerted them!

The Lake of Pearl

A dragon and a phoenix were best friends. Together, they guarded a perfect, sparkling pearl. One day, a queen bee stole it and hid it in her hive. Later, she took the pearl out to show it to her friends. The dragon and phoenix saw its light from far away. They rushed there and yelled, 'That is our pearl!'
The queen was startled and it slipped from her hands. As it fell, it turned into a sparkling lake. The two friends saw what had happened and decided to stay near it as mountains. They both can still be seen guarding the lake of their pearl.

The Doe in the Box

A monkey was once selling a large wooden box for a hundred gold pieces. Moe, the deer, bought the box and took it home.
When he opened it, he was shocked to see a beautiful doe inside. Moe asked her, 'How did you get trapped inside this box?'
The doe said, 'I am the deer king's daughter. Some monkeys kidnapped me. I don't remember anything else.'
Moe took her back immediately.
Then he helped the king's guards to arrest the monkey who had sold him the box. The king was very grateful and rewarded the deer.

The Jealous Sisters

Once, there lived three hare sisters. The elder two sisters were very jealous of the youngest sister. One day, the elder two sisters quietly hid the youngest sister deep in the forest while she was sleeping.
When she woke up, she tried to find her way back. Soon, she saw a lion with a thorn in his paw. Instead of being scared, she pulled out the thorn.
The lion was very grateful and showed her the way back. But when the wicked sisters saw the lion, they were so scared that they ran away and never troubled the youngest sister again.

The Best Bridegroom

The lion king once invited animals from all the neighbouring forests for a feast. He said to his daughter, 'I want you to choose a bridegroom from amongst them.'
The princess asked her friend, the bear, 'How should I choose the best bridegroom?' The wise bear made a plan. That evening, the bear loosened the cord of the huge chandelier in the main hall. It was about to fall on the princess! The animals saw this, but were too scared to help.
Only one fox risked his life and saved the princess. That is how the princess chose her bridegroom!

The Butterfly's Love for the Ant

A butterfly once fell in love with a beautiful ant. But one day, the butterfly got caught up in a spider's web. He could no longer fly! Seeing him so sad, the king of the insects said, 'Wash your wings in the morning dew. Then light a lamp from a shooting star. That will solve all your problems.'
The butterfly did as he was told. No sooner had he washed his wings in dew that he could fly again. Later, when he lit a lamp from a shooting star, the ant turned into a beautiful butterfly. They both got married and lived happily together.

The Eagle and the Quail

Once, an eagle chased a sparrow into a bamboo grove. He was amazed to see many quails there. He quickly came up with a plan.

He pretended to dash to the ground in pain. The quails were kind and took good care of him. But when they were not looking, he would quietly eat one of them. Finally, only one quail was left. The eagle said, 'Quail, let's be friends.' The quail said, 'You were friends with my brothers and sisters, and ate them up. How can an eagle and quail be friends?'

Saying this, the wise quail flew away.

The Tiger and the Crane

Once, a crane found a tiger cub in the forest. She felt sorry for him and raised him along with her own chick. The two young ones grew up and became good friends.

One day, a new crane came to the forest and bullied the young crane. The young crane cried out for help. The tiger rushed to help him. Following his natural instincts, he gobbled up the bully crane. He liked the taste of the crane very much indeed! The young crane saw this and flew away, saying, 'Brother, before you try to eat me, I should go away!'

Saying so, the crane flew away for he knew that he could become the tiger's food.

The Kangaroo and his Friends

A kangaroo had a beautiful garden. One day, he was unwell. So he asked the monkeys, who lived near his house, to water the plants.

The monkey chief told the others, 'Before you water the plants, lift them up. If their roots go deep, give plenty of water. If they have tiny roots, give little water.'

The foolish monkeys uprooted each plant to see the size of their roots and watered them above the ground!

When the kangaroo saw them, he shouted, 'What are you doing! My garden is ruined!'

The monkeys replied, 'We are doing exactly what our chief had told us!'

The kangaroo realised that the monkey chief was a fool and that he cannot be trusted.

The Wicked Hermit

A wicked hermit once came to live in a forest near a little lizard's house.

The lizard thought, 'It is such a good thing that a holy man has come to live here.' He went inside and saluted the hermit, respectfully. This became a daily ritual.

A few weeks later, the hermit was tired of eating fruits and started eating animals. One day, he thought, 'Lizard flesh must be tasty. Tomorrow I'll eat that little lizard.'

But the lizard heard of his evil plans. He quickly ran away, saying, 'You are a wicked man! Your holiness is just a show!'

The Monkeys and the Fish

Once, it rained very heavily for several days in the forest.
So, a group of monkeys had climbed up to the tree tops to save themselves. When the rain stopped, they looked down at the fish swimming in the water below.
A monkey said, 'The fish are going to drown.'
Soon the monkeys had lifted the fish out of the water and put them carefully on dry land.
Then, a monkey said, 'They were tired so they are sleeping.'
Another monkey said, 'When they wake up, they will be very grateful.'
The foolish monkeys never knew that the fish were all dead.

The Squirrel and the Tortoise

A squirrel and a tortoise lived near a river. One day, the squirrel wanted to eat berries that grew on the other side of the river. He could not swim, but he had an idea.
He said, 'Tortoise, you are the fastest among all the animals that live in this river. How I wish I could travel like you do!'
The tortoise was pleased and said, 'Hop on my back for a ride.'
The squirrel agreed. When they had reached the shore, the squirrel said, 'I only praised you because I wanted to cross the river.'
The tortoise never trusted the squirrel again.

Naughty Andrew

Andrew the panda loved apple pies. 'Mom, make another one,' was his request daily. Mother happily made the pies for him.
Once, Uncle Peter was coming to visit.
'Andrew, I am making a pie for Uncle Peter. Do not eat it!' said mother panda, sternly.
'Yes, mom,' said Andrew. But as soon as he saw the freshly baked pie, he forgot his promise! Within minutes, he had eaten the whole pie! Just then, mother entered the kitchen. She saw the crumbs on Andrew's shirt and realised what had happened.
She was very angry. She punished Andrew by not giving him any pies for a month! Poor Andrew learnt his lesson. He never broke his promise again.

The Foolish Monkey

A naughty monkey lived near the river. One day, he saw the fisherman casting his net into the river.
A little later, the fisherman went off to eat his lunch, leaving his nets there. The monkey immediately ran there. He too tried to cast the nets like he had seen the fisherman do. But poor monkey got trapped in the net himself and fell into the river!
'Help!' he cried. 'Please save me!'
Luckily, the fisherman came back just then and saved the monkey. The monkey was very grateful and promised never to do such naughty things again.

The Soft Red Ball

Two bear cubs loved playing on the hill.
One day, they found a soft red ball there and started playing with it.
But when they rolled the ball down the hill, the ball grew smaller and smaller.
The cubs asked their aunt, the owl, about the ball. But she did not know why it became small.
They asked their cousin, the wolf, but he did not know either.
Finally, their wise uncle, the elephant, said, 'This ball is made of wool. As you rolled it down the hill, it left a trail of string behind and thus became small.' Thus, the mystery was solved.

The Magical Paint Brush

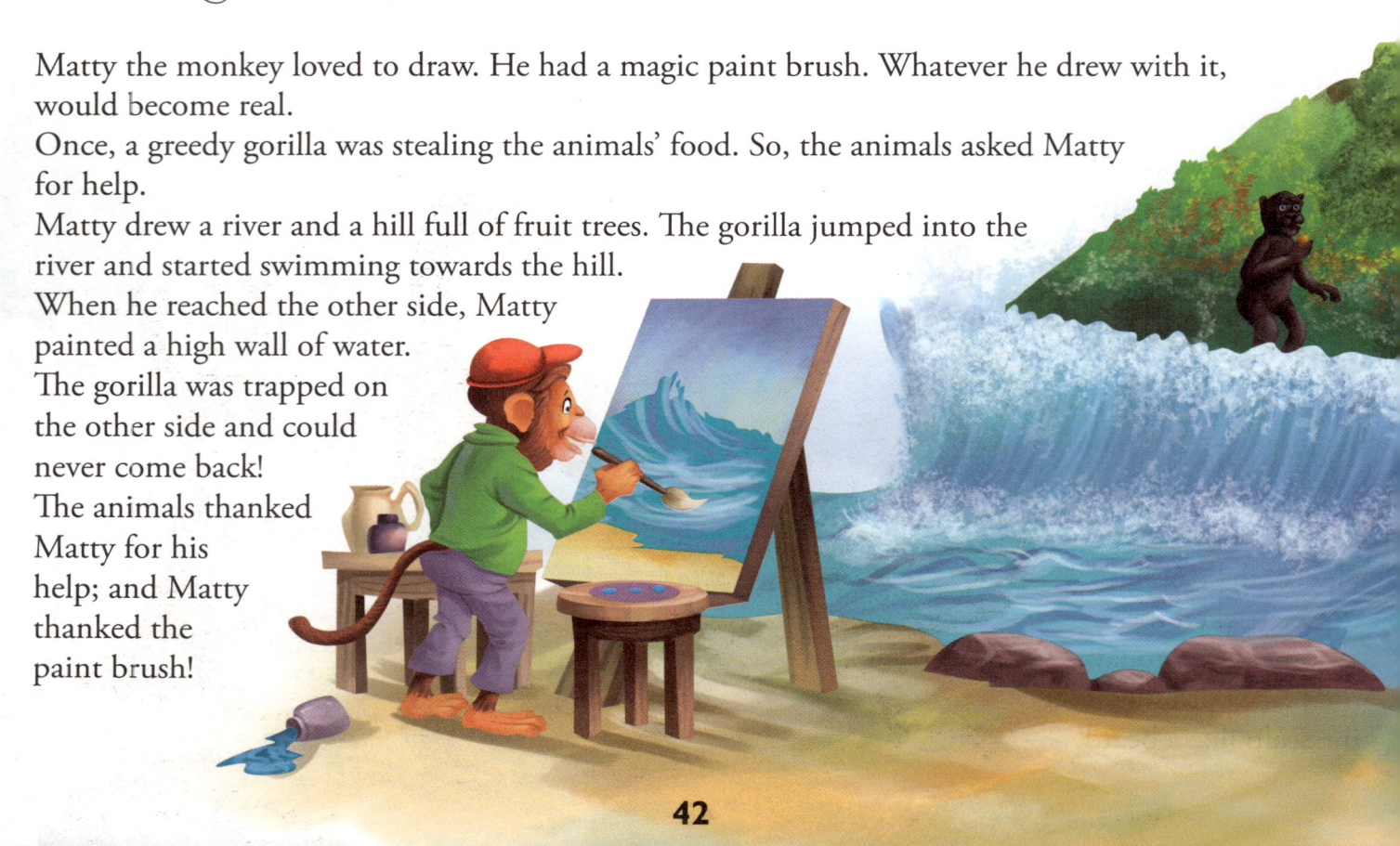

Matty the monkey loved to draw. He had a magic paint brush. Whatever he drew with it, would become real.
Once, a greedy gorilla was stealing the animals' food. So, the animals asked Matty for help.
Matty drew a river and a hill full of fruit trees. The gorilla jumped into the river and started swimming towards the hill.
When he reached the other side, Matty painted a high wall of water.
The gorilla was trapped on the other side and could never come back!
The animals thanked Matty for his help; and Matty thanked the paint brush!

The Most Beautiful Baby

Long ago, baby birds were sent to 'Bird School'. If they were naughty, they were not given any food. When father owl heard this, he decided to sneak some food in for his baby. On the way, he met mother partridge, who said, 'Please give my baby some food, too. He is the most beautiful child. You will know him immediately.' However, father owl could not find any child more beautiful than his own. So, mother partridge's baby remained hungry!

When mother partridge heard this, she exclaimed, 'I should have known! Every parent thinks his child is the most beautiful!'

The Turkey and his Beard

A terrapin was returning home from war. He was wearing the enemy's scalp around his neck. 'You look so funny!' laughed a turkey, 'Come, let me show you how to wear it properly.'

The terrapin wanted to look good, so he gave the scalp to the turkey. The turkey put it around his neck, near the chin, so that it looked like a beard. Then he quickly ran away, still wearing it. The terrapin tried to catch him, but he could not. Hence, the clever turkey tricked the terrapin. Even today, the turkey proudly wears the scalp like a beard.

The Cheat Rice-Seller

A magpie went to buy rice. But the rice-seller lark was a cheat. His assistant filled half her bag with sand and half with rice. At home, the magpie realised that the lark had tricked her. She quickly sifted out the rice. Then, she took back the bag of sand to the rice-seller.

She had thought of a plan to trick him. She reached the shop and said, 'I found sand mixed with the rice. But when I sifted the rice, I found gold in the sand!'

'Give me back that bag and take your money,' said the greedy lark. With the money, the magpie returned home. Meanwhile, the lark wanted to find gold! But there was no gold in the sand! Thus, the cheater was cheated.

The Wolf and the Dancing Goat

A young goat was left behind by a goatherd. A wolf saw him and started chasing him. Realising that he would not be seen by the hounds the goat thought of a plan to save itself.

He said, 'Dear wolf, I am sure you will eat me. But I have a wish before I die. Will you please whistle a tune so that I may dance?'

The wolf agreed. He began to whistle loudly and the goat started dancing. But the goatherd's hounds also heard the whistling and ran there at once, barking loudly.

'I should have just eaten you instead of trying to please you,' said the wolf before running away.

Lost and Found

One day, Mummy rhinoceros was frantically searching everywhere for her keys. 'Where can I have kept the house keys!' she wondered. Mummy rhinoceros had to take her baby to a very important doctor's appointment but could not leave without locking the door. Suddenly, she heard a distinctive 'cling, cling' of the keys. Mummy followed the noise and the sight in front of her made her burst out laughing.
Baby rhinoceros was crawling with the keys half hanging out from his diaper pants. When he sat down the keys rattled! The keys were found! Mummy rhinoceros realised that in her haste, she had not seen the keys even though they were right in front of her. That is why we should never try to do anything in haste!

The Otter and the Bear

Once, an otter could not catch any fish. He was about to go home disappointed, when a bear came and asked him for some honey. The otter gave him honey. The bear then dipped his paw in the honey and went to the river with insects circling around his honey-coated paw. He dipped his paw in the river and the fish were attracted by the insects. Then, the bear caught the fish easily! The bear ate some fish and left some behind. He said to the otter, 'These fish are for you. They are in return for your honey.' The happy otter thanked the bear and then hurried back home to cook the fish!

The Drop of Honey

A bear once saw a beehive on a tree. He filled the honey into his water-bag and went back to a fox's grocery shop to sell it. Just outside the shop, a drop of honey fell on the ground. Some flies gathered around it. A bird swooped down upon the flies. A cat saw the excitement and jumped on the bird. The bear and the fox tried to stop the commotion. But the bear slipped on the fallen honey and accidentally stepped on the fox's tail. Thus, they started fighting, too.

A wise owl saw this and said, 'Don't fight for a drop of honey!'

The bear and the fox realised that they were being foolish and stopped fighting at once!

The Simple Life

A traveller pelican once met a small tribe of fowls and said, 'I am curious about your way of life.'

The fowl king replied, 'Long ago, we adopted a simple way of life and have followed it ever since. We have no interest in wealth, as it doesn't last. We bury the dead in front of our houses to remind us about the reality of death. We don't kill animals, and we eat grass. Most importantly, we never forget about God.'

The pelican was very impressed. Wherever he went, he spread the message of peace as taught by the fowls.

The Blind Vulture

A blind vulture lived on a tree. He looked after the children of the other birds, and in return, they fed him.

One day, a cat came there and said, 'I have vowed not to kill any animal or bird. I heard that you are a wise bird. Therefore, I am here to learn from you.'

The vulture was flattered and allowed her to live there. But the sly cat ate up many young birds and then quietly left. The birds blamed the vulture for trusting the cat and stopped feeding him. Now he was sorry for his foolishness, but it was too late.

The Father and the Son

A hyena and his cub went to drink water from a river. The cub wanted to swim in the river and pleaded, 'Father, please let me swim.'
But the hyena warned him that it was dangerous and said, 'No, son.'
But when the hyena was not looking, the cub jumped into the water. At first, he enjoyed himself. But soon, he got tired and could not swim anymore in the strong current. Scared, he let out a cry.
The hyena heard the cry, jumped into the water and saved his son. When they reached the bank, the cub cried and promised to never disobey his father again.

The Naughty Baby-Bear

A naughty baby-bear lived with his parents. Once, he wandered into the forest and got lost. He climbed up a high tree, but he could see no one.
Also, he did not know how to come down from the tree! So he kept sitting at the top, crying softly.
A lion heard him cry and said, 'Come down. I will help you find your parents.'
But baby-bear did not trust him. A little later, he saw an old elephant and asked for help. With his long trunk, the elephant lifted him down. He put baby-bear on his back and took him back home.

The Mongoose and the Snake

A mongoose once saved a snake's life. The grateful snake said, 'I promise, I will repay your kindness.' Some days later, the mongoose had to go away for work. So he asked the snake, 'Please take care of my children.'
But the wicked snake ate up the mongoose's children. Then he pretended that he knew nothing about them. When he returned, the mongoose realised his mistake of trusting the snake. He was very upset and attacked the snake. He said, 'We can never be friends from now on.'
To this day, the mongoose attacks the snake when he sees him.

Birds of a Flock

Once, a group of hungry mynahs went to a grain field and ate their favourite food. But suddenly a big net fell on them, catching them unawares.
It was a wolf's net and he laughed, 'Aha! I have fooled you.'
But the mynahs' leader was very clever. He said to the mynahs, 'Our strength is in our numbers. Everyone start flapping your wings fast and rise in the air.' Immediately, they rose very high, with the bird net, away from the wolf. The group flew far away and then flew out from under the net one by one, saving themselves.

Why Lizards Cannot Sit Upright

Long ago, lizards sat upright. Then one day, a frog and a lizard passed a high fence. On the other side, there was a pond surrounded by green grass.
'The pond must be full of insects to eat! Let's go there right now!' exclaimed the lizard.
They first tried climbing over the fence but it was very high. 'Let's try to squeeze through that narrow crack near the ground!' the frog said.
The lizard struggled to get through the crack. But alas!
Just then, a rail fell down and squashed his back flat.
Since that time, lizards can never sit upright.

Lazy Lizzie

Lizzie was a lazy lizard. She did not like to help around the house. Her father would say, 'Lizzie, help your mother.' But Lizzie would keep sleeping.
Once, Lizzie's mother fell ill and father had to go away for work. Lizzie had to do everything alone. Working from morning to night, she took care of mother, cooked food and even cleaned the house. She realized how hard her mother worked everyday.
Two days later when father came home, Lizzie said, 'Mother works very hard at home. I promise I will help around the house more so that she does not fall ill again.'
Lizzie was never lazy again!

How the White Hen Got Speckles

Once, a white hen went to meet a lion. She also carried a fox along in a basket. Soon, they met a river, which said, 'Please take me along.' The white hen agreed. The river hopped into the basket too.
A little further, they met fire, who became ashes and jumped into the basket, too.
But when they reached the lion's palace, the guards captured the white hen. The fox, river and fire decided to rescue her. As they jumped out of the basket, some ash fell on the white hen and could never be washed off! That is how, the hen got speckled!

The Jackdaw and the Doves

A cunning jackdaw saw a family of doves with a lot of food. He painted himself white and joined them in order to share their food. As long as the jackdaw was quiet, the doves thought he was one of them and let him stay in their cote.
But, when one day he began to chatter, they drove him out. The jackdaw thought, 'Alas, no more food from the doves. Let me go back to my flock.'
Sadly, his flock did not recognise him because of his white colour. Thus, the jackdaw had no family to live with any more!

Water Turtles

Years ago, turtles lived only on land with the other animals. One day, some wolves caught a turtle.
The turtle said, 'To get my meat, you need to remove my shell. How will you do that?'
The wolves replied, 'We will break the shell with stones.'
The turtle said, 'It will take you a long time to break it. Instead, throw me in the water. The shell will become soft and will be easier to break.'
But when the wolves did this, the turtle swam away! He then decided to live safely in water and all the other turtles followed him as well. And that is why turtles live in water.

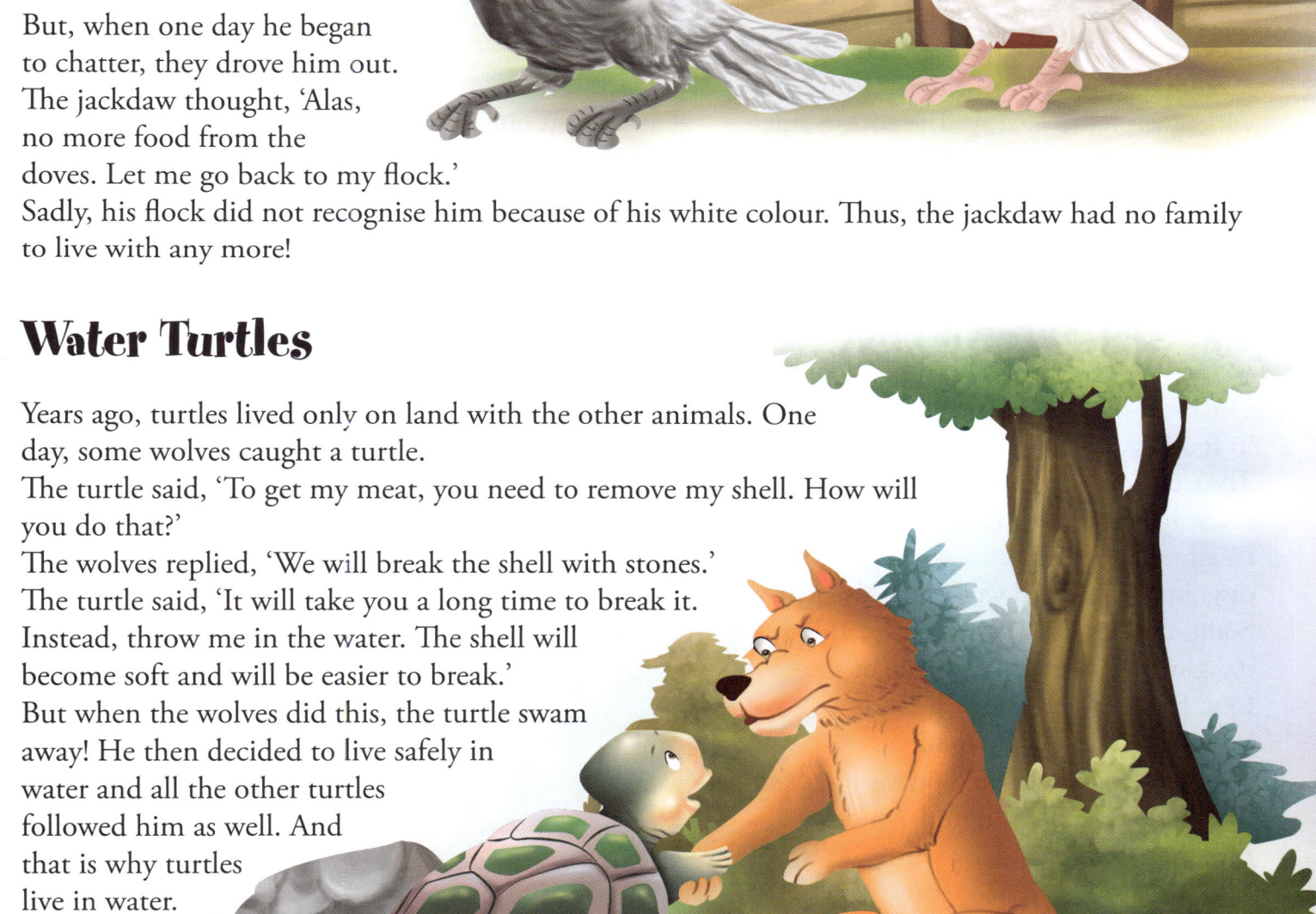

The Cotton Ghost

Once August the cat went to his in-laws' house. He was served delicious food for dinner. August felt shy, so he ate very little.

But at midnight, he felt hungry and went to the kitchen. He ate some honey, which it dripped all over him and on the floor.

Suddenly, August slipped and fell with a loud noise. Hearing the noise, his father-in-law woke up. Scared, August fell on white cotton wool which was lying nearby. The cotton stuck to the honey on him and he looked exactly like a ghost! Everyone screamed when they saw him, until he managed to explain what had happened. Then they all had a good laugh and went back to bed. But August learnt his lesson and was never so shy again.

The Daughter's Love

Once, an elephant asked his daughter how much she loved him. She said, 'I love you as much as salt in food.'

The elephant was furious hearing this and threw her out of the house. However, his daughter loved her father very much. So, she disguised herself and worked in his kitchen. Soon, the elephant held a party. The daughter made sure that none of the food had salt in it and as a result, no guest could eat the food.

The elephant finally realised the importance of salt and understood that his daughter did love him very much.

After the party, the elephant's daughter removed her disguise. The delighted elephant hugged her and never questioned his daughter's love again.

The Hart and the Vine

One day, a hart, chased by wolves, ran for a very long time but the wolves did not stop following him. He was so tired that he hid beneath the large leaves of a vine. The wolves did not see behind the vine and overlooked the hart's place of hiding. The hart assumed that the wolves had left and started nibbling on the leaves of the vine. But a wolf who was at the back of the pack heard the rustling of the leaves and looked back. He saw the hart and attacked him.

The hart cried out, 'It serves me right! I should not have eaten the vine that had saved me.'

Hani, the Proud Peacock

Hani was a very thoughtless and silly peacock. One day, Hani saw a rabbit working in his garden. He asked, 'What are you doing?'

The rabbit replied, 'I am planting carob seeds.'

Hani asked, 'How many years would it take for the trees to grow?'

The rabbit replied that it would take seventy years! Hani was astonished. He said, 'You are foolish. You will not even live for seventy years!'

The rabbit said, 'My grandfather planted carob trees for me. I am doing the same for my grandchildren.'

Hani was impressed by the rabbit's foresight. Inspired by the rabbit, he too began to plan for the future.

The Lame Donkey

A farmer's donkey was grazing in the fields. Suddenly, he saw a wolf coming towards him. So, he acted as if he were lame. The wolf asked, 'What is wrong with your leg?' The clever donkey replied, 'Oh! I was walking through a bush when a sharp thorn pricked my foot.' He added, 'You can eat me if you want. But the thorn may injure your throat, so pull it out from my foot first.'
The wolf lifted up the donkey's foot and searched for the thorn. Right then, the donkey kicked the wolf's mouth and ran away to safety.

The Hawk and the Chickens

A long time ago, a hawk and a hen were engaged. But a cock also loved the hen and wanted to marry her.
One day, the cock went to the hen's house and called out to her. The hen recognised him and went for a walk with him.
When the hawk saw this, he was angry. He cancelled the marriage and asked for his gifts back. But the hen's parents had already used up the gifts.
The hawk was very angry and chased the hens all over the place! In fact, even today if a hawk sees a hen, he tries to chase it and get back its gifts!

Brave Sarah

Little Clara was the newest member of the buffalo herd. Everyone loved her and looked after her.
Once while drinking water, a lion, who had been waiting to catch the youngest of the herd, pounced on little Clara. She screamed, 'Please, help me!'
Clara's elder sister, Sarah was drinking water close by. She heard Clara shout and thought, 'I can't let that lion eat my little sister!'
Sarah immediately raised her horns and charged towards the lion, bellowing loudly. The lion was startled by the sudden noise and ran away. Little Clara was safe! Everyone praised Sarah for her bravery.

The Fox Meets his Match

A cock perched on a tall tree crowed loudly. A hungry fox heard the crowing and thought of a way to eat the cock.
He said, 'Did you hear that peace has been declared among all beasts and birds? Come down and let's discuss it.'
The clever cock replied, 'I see a pack of hounds coming this way.'
'Oh, I must run,' said the fox.
'Stop, surely you are not afraid of hounds in these days of peace!' said the cock.
'No, but I don't know if they have heard the announcement yet,' the fox said and ran away quickly.

The Jealous Sparrow

An eagle flew down and carried away a lamb to eat it. A sparrow saw the eagle and thought, 'If the eagle can do it, then I can carry a sheep for my lunch too.' The foolish sparrow flew down and landed on a sheep to lift it, her feet got stuck in the thick wool. The herd's owner was a bear. He thought, 'A bird just carried away my lamb. I will punish this one.' He hit the sparrow. The poor sparrow cried, "I am a small bird and should have been happy with the little food that I get."

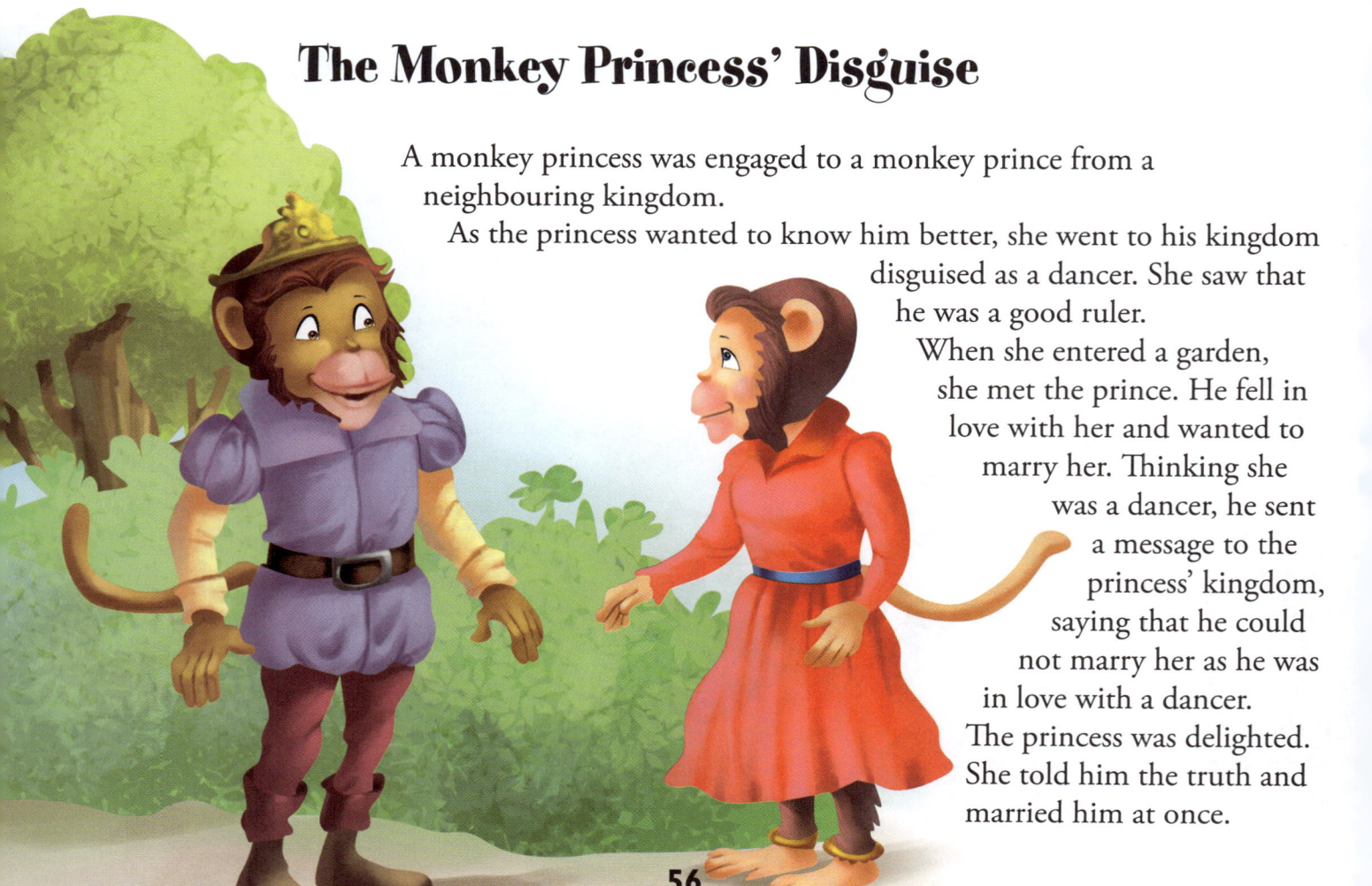

The Monkey Princess' Disguise

A monkey princess was engaged to a monkey prince from a neighbouring kingdom.

As the princess wanted to know him better, she went to his kingdom disguised as a dancer. She saw that he was a good ruler.

When she entered a garden, she met the prince. He fell in love with her and wanted to marry her. Thinking she was a dancer, he sent a message to the princess' kingdom, saying that he could not marry her as he was in love with a dancer.

The princess was delighted. She told him the truth and married him at once.

The Swallows and the Snake

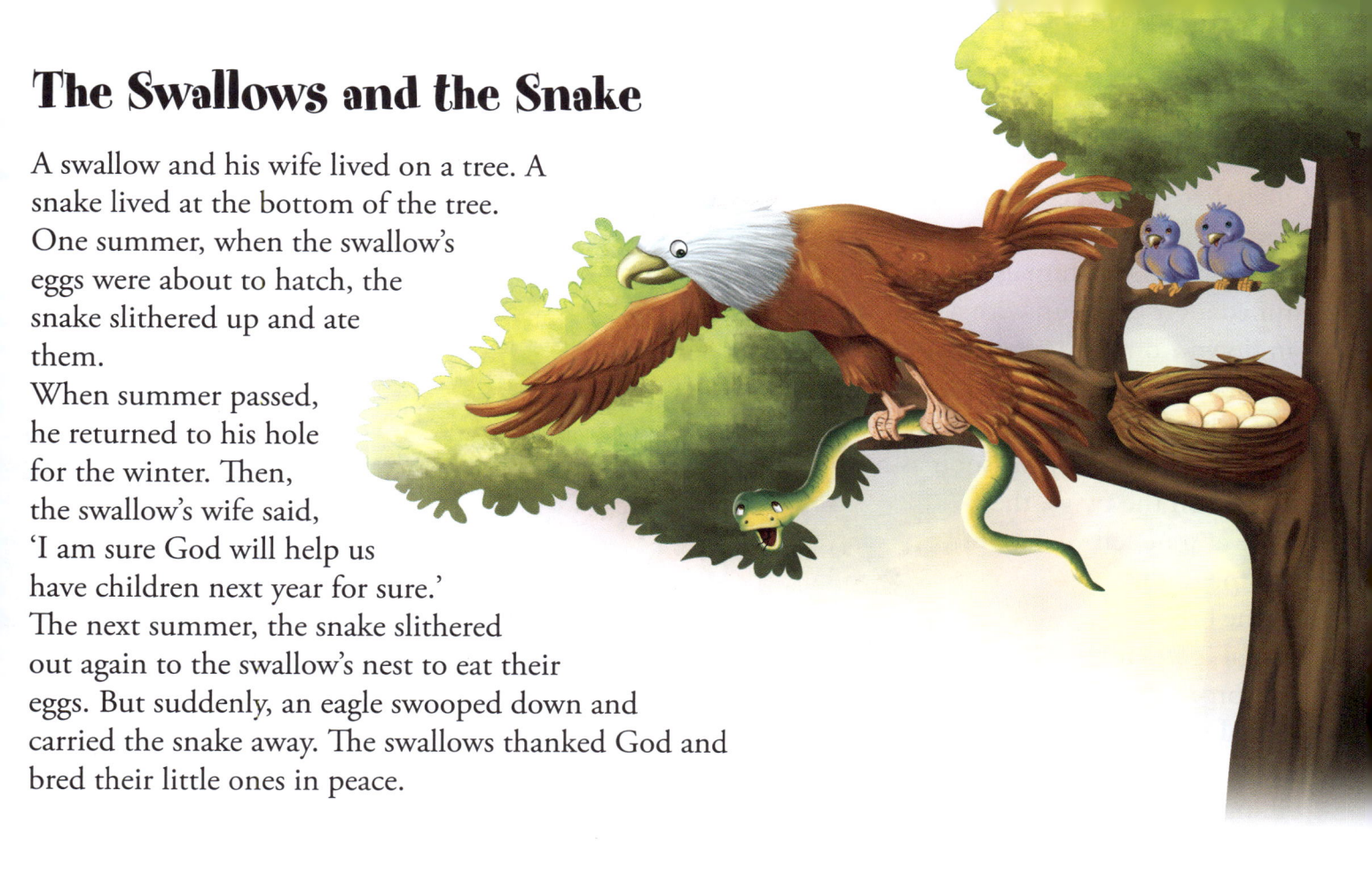

A swallow and his wife lived on a tree. A snake lived at the bottom of the tree. One summer, when the swallow's eggs were about to hatch, the snake slithered up and ate them.
When summer passed, he returned to his hole for the winter. Then, the swallow's wife said, 'I am sure God will help us have children next year for sure.'
The next summer, the snake slithered out again to the swallow's nest to eat their eggs. But suddenly, an eagle swooped down and carried the snake away. The swallows thanked God and bred their little ones in peace.

The Unemployed Jackals

Three lazy jackals spent their days looking for leftovers. Once, they found nothing to eat for three days.
They tried, but could not get any jobs. Finally, they decided to ask the king for help.
The king heard their story patiently and then said, 'You say that you have no food and no jobs. But you must realise that you will only get jobs if you are willing to work hard and not be lazy.'
The jackals realised that it was their own bad habits that had led them to starvation. Seeing that they really wanted to change, the king gave them jobs in his army. The jackals were never lazy again.

The Clever Monkey

Once there lived a clever monkey in the forest. One day, he saw that a new tiger had come to the forest. This tiger started attacking animals and hurting them. The monkey immediately came up with a plan to save the animals. He ran down from his tree and collected all the fallen twigs and branches that he could find. He laid them neatly over a deep ditch. Soon, the wicked tiger passed that way. As soon as he stepped on the twigs, they broke and he fell into the ditch! All the other animals gathered and forced the wicked tiger to leave the forest. The wicked tiger agreed willingly. The animals thanked the monkey and praised his intelligence.

The Two Parrots

Once, two baby parrots were blown away by a storm.
One parrot fell near a hyena's home, while the other fell near a hare's home. They grew up learning from what they saw.

One day, the hyena's parrot saw an elephant and started screaming to the hyenas, 'Kill him!' The elephant quickly escaped and reached the hare's home. There, the other parrot showed him great respect. The elephant was surprised and told him about the hyena's parrot.

'He is my brother, but he fell into bad company,' said the parrot. The elephant commented, 'Company has a great effect on our personality!' Saying so, he went away.

Panda Gummy

A long time ago, there lived a panda named Gummy. He was a very nice panda, but he did not want to go to school! Everyday, he would run away from school, sit in the bamboo grove and eat bamboo shoots all day long. One day, his friend Sherry wrote him a note: 'Dear Gummy, please come with me to the fair tomorrow.' But Gummy could not read! Thus, while all the other pandas were enjoying themselves at the fair, poor Gummy did not even know about it! The next day, Sherry asked Gummy why he had not come to the fair. When Gummy realised what had happened, he felt very bad. He realised that it was his own fault and stopped running away from school. He soon learnt to read and write just like the other pandas! He was happy now.

The Hare and the Coyotes

Two hares, Ace and Moe were friends. One day, Ace went on a journey. On the way, some wicked coyotes told him, 'Don't carry water! There is a lake ahead!' Ace believed them, but found no water at all! Exhausted, he slept and then the coyotes came and made a meal of him. When Ace did not return, Moe decided to look for him. He also met the same coyotes but he did not believe them.

Moe was alert and the wicked coyotes could not attack him. He also understood what must have happened to Ace. Moe thought sadly about his friend Ace and said, 'I wish you had been careful and didn't trust strangers.'

The Musical Jackal

Percy the jackal liked music very much. But his parents were always upset with him and said, 'You should learn to hunt, rather than play music all the time.'
One day, Percy was trying to hunt, when he saw a drum under a tree.
He forgot all about hunting! He softly tapped the drum and it made the sound, 'Dum-da-dum.'
Percy started tapping out different beats on the drum, and slowly many animals gathered there. They were all amazed at the music he was making. Soon, they all started dancing and enjoying the music of the drum! Percy became famous as the 'musical jackal'.
Animals from far and wide came to hear him play. His parents never called him useless anymore.

The Witty Old Owl

A blind owl made a bargain with a pigeon doctor. If the pigeon could cure her, only then would she pay his fees. But the greedy pigeon started stealing things from the blind owl's home. The owl did not know about this. Over time, the owl was cured, and she realised that the pigeon had been stealing things from her house when he came to cure her. She was angry and refused to pay his fees. Then, they took the matter to a falcon. The owl said, 'I promised to pay him if I could see. But I can't see all of my valuables. So I can't pay.'
The falcon understood what had happened and punished the pigeon for his greed.

Clever Suzy

One day, Suzy the vixen prepared chicken for a dinner party. When she was done, she asked her husband, 'When shall I serve the food?'
Suzy's husband said, 'I am sorry, dear. Our guests have not arrived yet, so please don't serve dinner just now.' Saying this, he rushed out of the house to ask his guests to hurry up.'
Suzy was tired and hungry by now. As she sat waiting for the guests, she decided to taste a little piece of the chicken. But it was so delicious that she kept eating, and before long, she had eaten the entire chicken!
Just then, the guests came. Suzy wondered what to do. Then she came up with a plan. She secretly told the guests, 'My husband is going to eat you all! Run away!'
The guests were scared and ran away. Thus, clever Suzy did not have to serve the chicken at all!

David's Mistake

David the little monkey had just started going to school. His teacher, Miss Mary the rhinoceros, had a kind heart and she loved David a lot.
But today, David was ashamed of himself. 'Everyone will laugh at me,' he thought, rushing towards home.
His mother was surprised to see him home this early. He whispered something in her ear.
Immediately, his mother hugged him and said, 'It is okay. Wetting pants is something that happens to all small children. You did not do it intentionally.'
Relieved that it was not a big mistake, David changed his clothes and went back to school happily.

Hamy and the Oasis

Hamy, the camel, had been travelling across the desert for three days and his store of water was almost over. Luckily, at sunset, he saw a small oasis. He had found water at last! But a huge sand monster suddenly covered the oasis and said, 'If you can find the oasis within one hour, you can have the water. Otherwise I will eat you up.'

Hamy cleverly charged right at the sand monster and attacked him. The monster was so surprised at this bold attack, that he moved away, uncovering the oasis! Thus, the sand monster lost and Hamy drank as much water as he wanted!

Abe and the Fish

Abe, the seal, once caught a huge fish. The other seals said, 'Surely the leader would like that fish!'

But while presenting the fish to his leader, Abe slipped! The basket and the fish fell out of his arms. The huge fish flew towards the leader's throne. There was a cry of surprise from all the other seals.

No one knew that a poisonous scorpion had been hiding behind the cushions of the throne. The fish hit the scorpion and killed him just in time, before he could bite the leader!

Seeing these strange turn of events, everyone was surprised. The leader thanked Abe and gave him many gifts.

Sally Salmon

Sally was the youngest salmon in the family. Whenever, she said to her brothers and sisters, 'Let's play!' they would say, 'Not now, we're busy.'

One day, tired of being told to go away, Sally thought, 'I will play alone under this big rock.'

After playing for a while all by herself, she got tired and fell asleep.

Back home, mother salmon could not find Sally, and no one knew where she was. Worried, everyone immediately went looking for Sally. But no one could find her.

Meanwhile, Sally woke up in the evening. She became afraid as it was getting dark and so she rushed home.

Later, glad to see her safe, everyone hugged her tightly and promised to play with her for a little while, everyday.

The Parsley Queen

Alice, the rabbit loved her mother a lot. One day, Alice's mother asked her to pluck some parsley.

Just then, the king of rabbits passed by. All the rabbits gathered to catch a glimpse of the king. Only Alice continued to pluck parsley.

He saw Alice and thought, 'Why is this girl not eager to see me?'

So, he sent one of his guards to ask her what she was doing.

'I am here to pluck parsley for my mother. Therefore, I cannot spare a moment to see the king,' explained Alice. Sammy was impressed by her dedication and soon married her. And as the king had first seen her plucking parsley, Alice was also called the parsley queen!

The Greedy Lion

One day, a hungry lion saw a fat hare fast asleep near his burrow. When he was just about to pounce on the hare, he saw a doe passing by. He left the hare and went after the doe. Scared by the sudden noise, the hare woke up and hopped away, quickly. Meanwhile, the lion was unable to catch the doe and returned to his den to feed himself on the hare. Seeing that the hare had also run away, he sadly thought, 'It serves me right for being greedy and running after a larger animal when I could have easily had a good meal.'

The Camel, the Elephant and the Monkey

Once, the animals were trying to elect the bravest animal among them. The camel and the elephant were the foremost candidates as they were bigger and stronger compared to the other animals.

Then a monkey came forward and said, 'The camel and the elephant cannot be considered the bravest of all!' He continued, 'The camel does not even get angry at those who mistreat him while the elephant is afraid of a small fly as it can kill him instantly when it enters his ears!' Hearing this, both the camel and the elephant withdrew from the competition! And so, once again the search for the bravest animal started.

The Gnat and the Lion

A gnat once stung a sleeping lion on his nostrils. The lion woke up and was very furious. He wanted to crush the gnat with his paws. But while trying to catch him, the lion bruised himself with his sharp claws.

Meanwhile, every time he escaped the lion's blow, the gnat felt as if he had defeated the lion. In his happiness, he did not see where he was going, and got trapped in a spider's web. Lamenting on his fate and approaching death, the gnat said, 'I can win against a huge beast like a lion, yet I will die in a small insect's trap!'

Domi and his Cat

Domi the bear was so poor that he had to sell all his belongings to get enough food to eat. The only thing he never sold was his cat.

One day, the cat said to him, 'You have been kind to me. I will solve all our problems.' So, the cat caught a thief who had stolen the king's gold and told the guards, 'My master Domi had caught the thief.' The pleased lion called Domi and decided to marry his daughter to him. Soon, Domi and the lioness princess were married. Domi was now happy because of his kindness to his cat!

The Lion and the Bull

Once, a lion and wanted to eat a bull. But he was afraid of the bull's great size and decided to trick him.
The lion said, 'Friend, please come to my den and share a dinner of fresh vegetables with me!' He hoped to attack the bull there. The bull agreed. When he came to the den in the evening, the bull looked around the cave and left without saying a word. The lion asked him what happened.
As the bull rushed away, he answered, 'I saw that you have no vegetables for dinner. I understood that I was to be your dinner!' The smart bull had managed to save himself.

The Turkey With a Beautiful Heart

A turkey and a peacock were best friends. However, the turkey always thought, 'I wish I was as pretty as the peacock and had such beautiful feathers!'
Once, while playing, the peacock's long feathers became tangled in a fence. 'Someone please help. My feathers are breaking!' cried the peacock. The turkey patiently took out all the feathers one by one and freed the peacock. The grateful peacock said, 'I am so glad that you are my friend. Your own feathers got torn while helping me but you did not stop. You truly have the most beautiful heart.' After that day, the turkey did not wish to have feathers like the peacock.

The Elephant With Magical Powers

Once, an old elephant had magical powers. One summer, there was no rain. The animals could not think of what to do, so they asked him to help them.
So, the elephant prayed to the rain gods and it started raining! After the rains, a big lake was formed.
The old elephant asked the animals to go fishing in the lake. The animals asked, 'From where would fish come in the lake?'
The elephant just smiled. The animals decided to try fishing. Soon, their nets carried all kinds of fish!
The animals realised that the elephant was a great magical being, and thanked him for all his help. The animals now had plenty to eat.

The Penguin who was Scared of Snow

Peter Penguin was afraid of snow. He was scared of falling and getting hurt. So, Peter's friends laughed at him. They called him 'Scaredy cat!'
His parents patiently explained, 'Peter, being a penguin you cannot be scared of ice. It is where you live.' But Peter was unable to overcome his fear.
One day while sleeping, he rolled off into the snow. It was fun and he did not get hurt! Later, he thought, 'How foolish I was to be scared of snow.'
And so, he kept sliding on the ice happily. Next day, Peter surprised everyone by bravely sliding down the highest ice slide. His parents were happy to see him.

Strange Friendship

Once, a rat saw a scared eaglet stuck in a vulture's net. The vulture was boiling water in a pot to cook the eaglet. Feeling sorry for the baby bird, the rat bit the net, freeing the eaglet. The eaglet's relieved mother said, 'Thank you dear rat, I will remember your kindness.'

A few days later, a fox caught the rat in his mouth and was taking him home to eat. The rat cried for help. Immediately, the eagle swooped down, picked up the fox and shook him hard. The scared fox dropped the rat, who ran away, thanking the eagle.

The Wolf-Stag

One day, a handsome stag came from a different forest to play with a herd of deer. A doe in the herd fell in love with him. She ran after him when he took his leave, hoping to follow him home. The stag said, 'Do not come after me, otherwise you will get hurt.' But she refused to listen to him. He started running, but she ran equally fast. As the moon came up, the stag changed into a wolf and shouted, 'I am a wolf but cursed to be a stag during the day! Run, or I will have to eat you!'

The doe finally ran away and saved herself.

The Vain Peacock

A peacock was very proud of his beautiful feathers. He would prance around saying, 'None of you are as pretty as me!'
The birds were tired of his vanity and went to the wise owl for advice. He said that he would take care of the problem if they sent the peacock to him. They did so.
Seeing him, the wise owl said, 'You are so proud of your feathers. But you have not done anything special. Your feathers are a gift from God. What are you so proud of?'
Hearing this, the peacock was very surprised. He had never thought this way before. He realised that the wise owl was speaking the truth. He finally stopped boasting, and became a much nicer creature!

The Elephant and his Blind Mother

Long ago, an elephant lived with his blind mother. He was a good son and took care of her with a lot of love.
One day, he was out gathering food for her, when a lion attacked him. The lion was hungry and wanted to eat the elephant. But the elephant said, 'I will meet you here tomorrow and fight with you. Right now, I must return home and feed my mother.'
The lion was stunned. He agreed, but followed the elephant home secretly. There, the lion was even more surprised to see the love with which the elephant took care of his mother. His hard heart softened and he decided not to harm the elephant. Thus, the elephant's love for his mother saved his life!

Movie Night

Lily, the wolf-cub, was going to see a movie with her mother. She had never seen a movie before.

Lily excitedly asked, 'How is it going to look? What will happen? Where will we see the movie?'

Mum just replied, 'Lily, have patience.'

Soon, they reached the movie hall. They sat on their seats with a big bag of popcorn. Suddenly, the lights went out and the movie started.

Lily thought it was a funny movie, and she loved it!

Lily got scared at times, and hid her head in her mother's arms. But mother always reminded her, 'It's just a movie, Lily.'

After the movie was over, Lily said, 'How wonderful it is that someone had thought of this whole story on their own, Mother. I want to grow up and write such stories too!'

Mum laughed and said, 'That is an excellent idea, Lily.'

The Kind and Hard Working Mouse

Once, the mouse chief invited all eligible mice to his house so that his daughter could choose the best bridegroom. Now, two mice brothers wanted to marry their chief's daughter. The elder brother was very clever and skilled. The younger brother was hard working and kind.

The chief's daughter noticed the two brothers and quickly made up her mind. She chose the younger brother to be her husband.

She explained, 'This mouse is both kind and hard working. He will always look after me and do what is best for me.'

Thus, they were married. The mouse chief was impressed by his daughter's decision.

The Best Soldier

Gon was a very special elephant. He was so strong that he could smash rocks! But he was very friendly and kind hearted, too. All the animals loved him because he was very nice to them.

As Gon grew up, he became stronger and stronger. But he was not happy, as he did not know what to do with all his strength! Then, one day, he met a fox who said, 'You are very strong and brave. You must come and meet the lion and join his army.'

Gon readily agreed and joined the lion's army. He was sent especially to fight dragons, wrestle evil bears and defeat them.

Thus, Gon finally found something to do that used his talents and abilities. He was no longer unhappy, and was glad to use his strength to help others!

A Day With Daddy at Work

Alan, the rhinoceros, was excited. His daddy worked at the science museum and was today taking him to a 'day-out at daddy's work'.

'Now, Alan, you can't just run around and scream in the museum,' warned daddy. Alan nodded.

In the Museum, Alan first visited the Archaeology Section and Arts Section. He liked the paintings and sculptures.

Then Daddy showed Alan the Science Section. Alan was curious to see a phone, electric bulb and the radio of the olden times.

Then they both watched a movie about the planets in the planetarium. 'It was awesome, daddy. Thank you!' said Alan happily in the evening.

Muss and Hector

Muss, the elephant was a grumpy king. He never laughed nor smiled. He even made a law that anyone who laughed should be arrested! Now, there lived a rabbit, Hector, who loved to laugh. He thought, 'I must change the king's mind.' The next day, Hector went up to the king and said seriously, 'Majesty, please allow me to present a play before you.'
Muss agreed. Everyone watched the play with much interest. Now the end of the story was very funny. It actually made Muss laugh!
He realised how nice it was to laugh and changed the law. Now, everyone in his kingdom was happy.

Wella, the Impatient Walrus

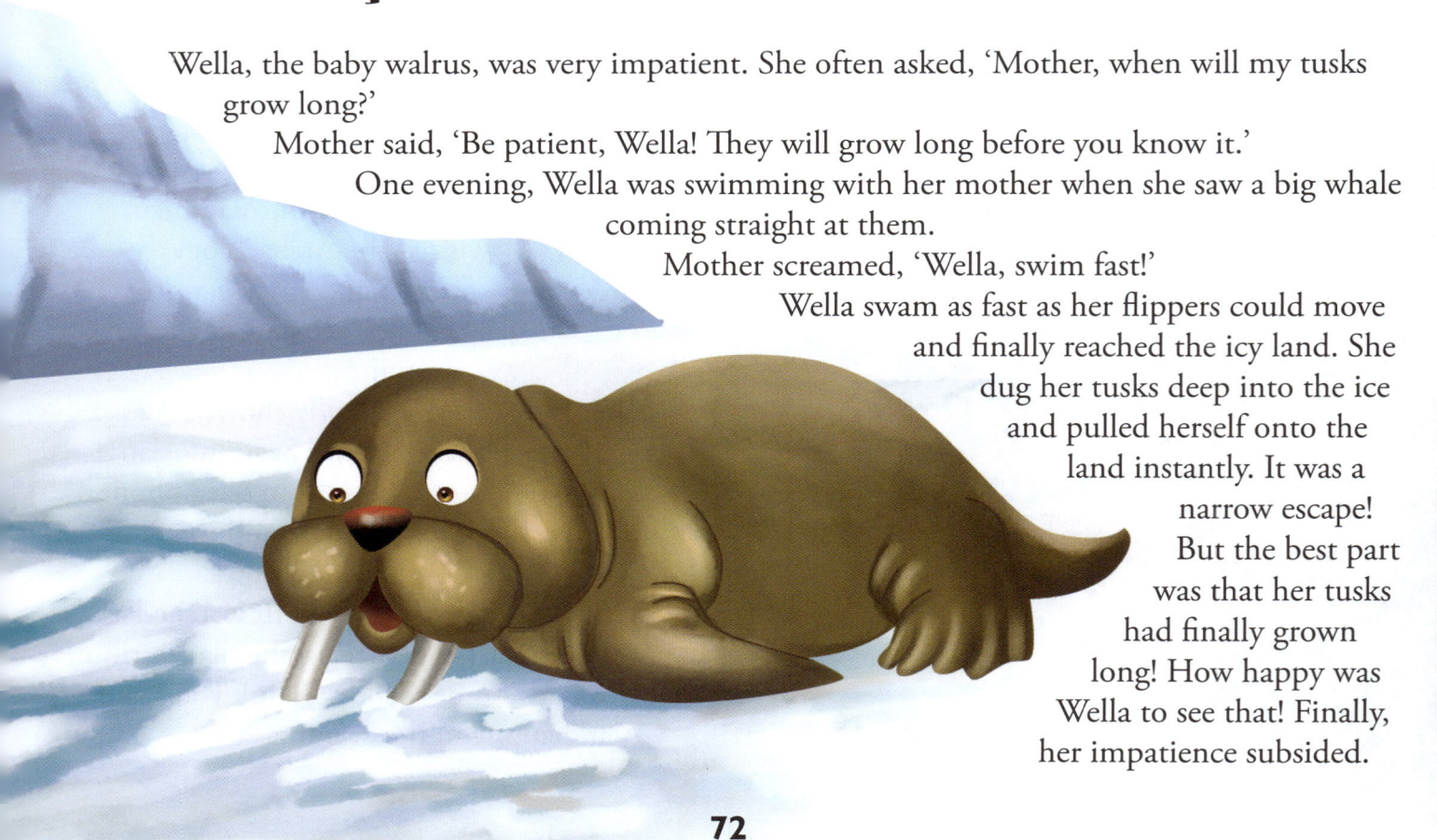

Wella, the baby walrus, was very impatient. She often asked, 'Mother, when will my tusks grow long?'

Mother said, 'Be patient, Wella! They will grow long before you know it.'

One evening, Wella was swimming with her mother when she saw a big whale coming straight at them.

Mother screamed, 'Wella, swim fast!'

Wella swam as fast as her flippers could move and finally reached the icy land. She dug her tusks deep into the ice and pulled herself onto the land instantly. It was a narrow escape! But the best part was that her tusks had finally grown long! How happy was Wella to see that! Finally, her impatience subsided.

The Kind Bear and the River God

Once, a kind bear put a fish that had jumped out of the river back into the water. This fish was actually the river god! Sometime later, the bear climbed onto a boat. Seeing how rich he looked, the boatman wolf stole the bear's money and threw him into the river. As the bear fell into the water, the river god saved him. Before the boat reached the bank, the bear had already reached the forest and complained to the lion about the wolf. The wolf was punished and the bear got all his money back. And that is how the river god paid for the bear's kindness.

The Poor Cat and the Rich Cat

Once, a poor cat met a well-fed, rich cat who said that she always ate good food. The poor cat asked her to share some of the extra food with him.

It was agreed that the poor cat would go to the rich cat's castle for some delicious food. The poor cat's mother said, 'Do not be so greedy. We are poor, but happy.'

But the poor cat would not listen. He went to the rich cat's place and waited for the food. But one day the castle's hounds saw the poor cat and drove him away. He understood what his mother meant, and decided never to be greedy again.

The Great King of the Forest

Once, a tiger attacked a fox. The fox cried out, 'How dare you attack the king of the forest?' The tiger looked at him in surprise and said, 'You are not a king!'

The clever fox said, 'All the animals run from me in terror! Come, I will show you.'

A deer saw the tiger walking behind the fox and ran away. Then, a group of monkeys saw them and fled, too.

The fox said, 'See how the animals flee at the very sight of me?'

The foolish tiger bowed low and said, 'Forgive me for attacking you, great king!'

The Unfair Vixen

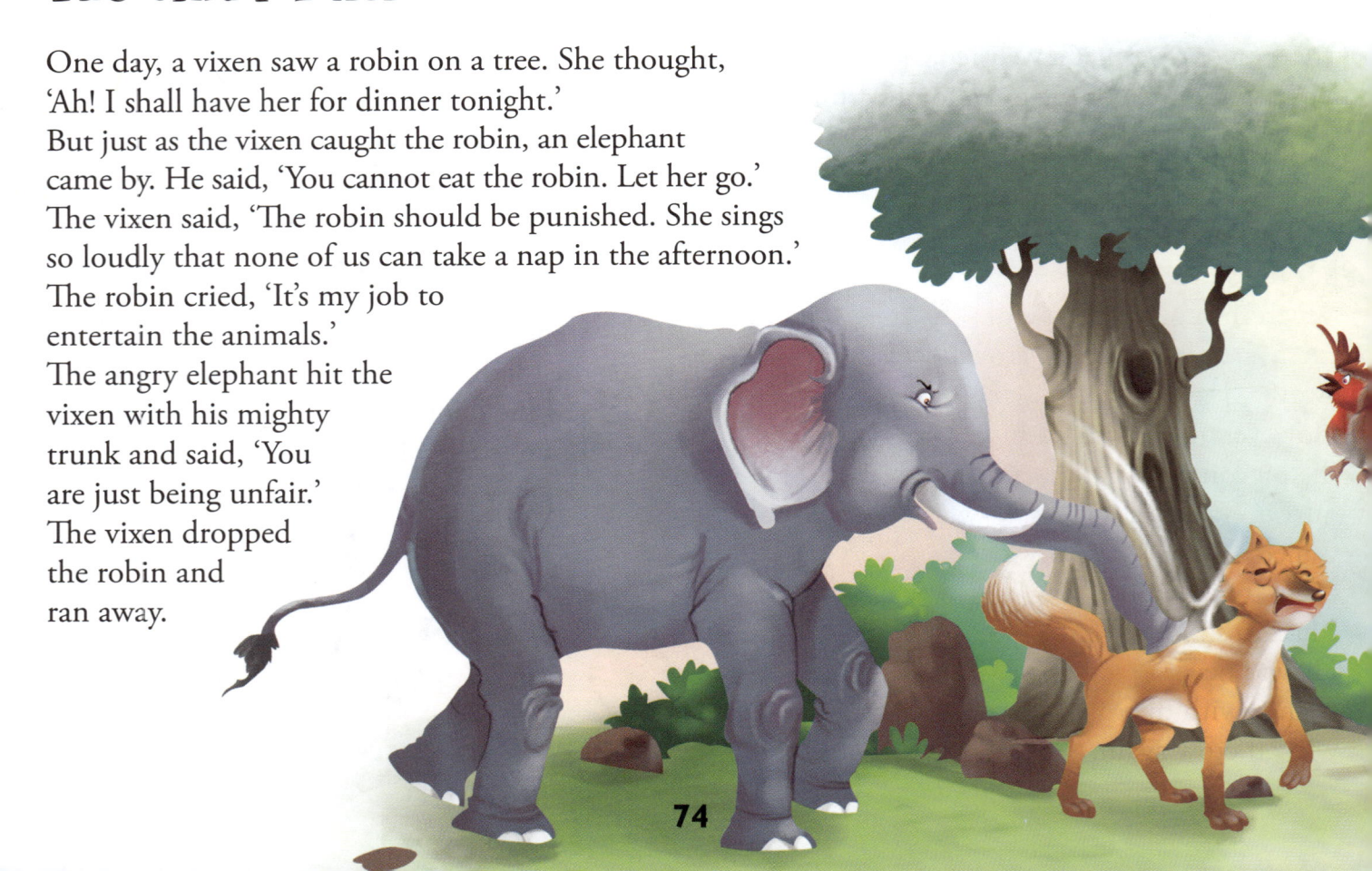

One day, a vixen saw a robin on a tree. She thought, 'Ah! I shall have her for dinner tonight.'

But just as the vixen caught the robin, an elephant came by. He said, 'You cannot eat the robin. Let her go.'

The vixen said, 'The robin should be punished. She sings so loudly that none of us can take a nap in the afternoon.'

The robin cried, 'It's my job to entertain the animals.'

The angry elephant hit the vixen with his mighty trunk and said, 'You are just being unfair.'

The vixen dropped the robin and ran away.

The Hawk and the Bear

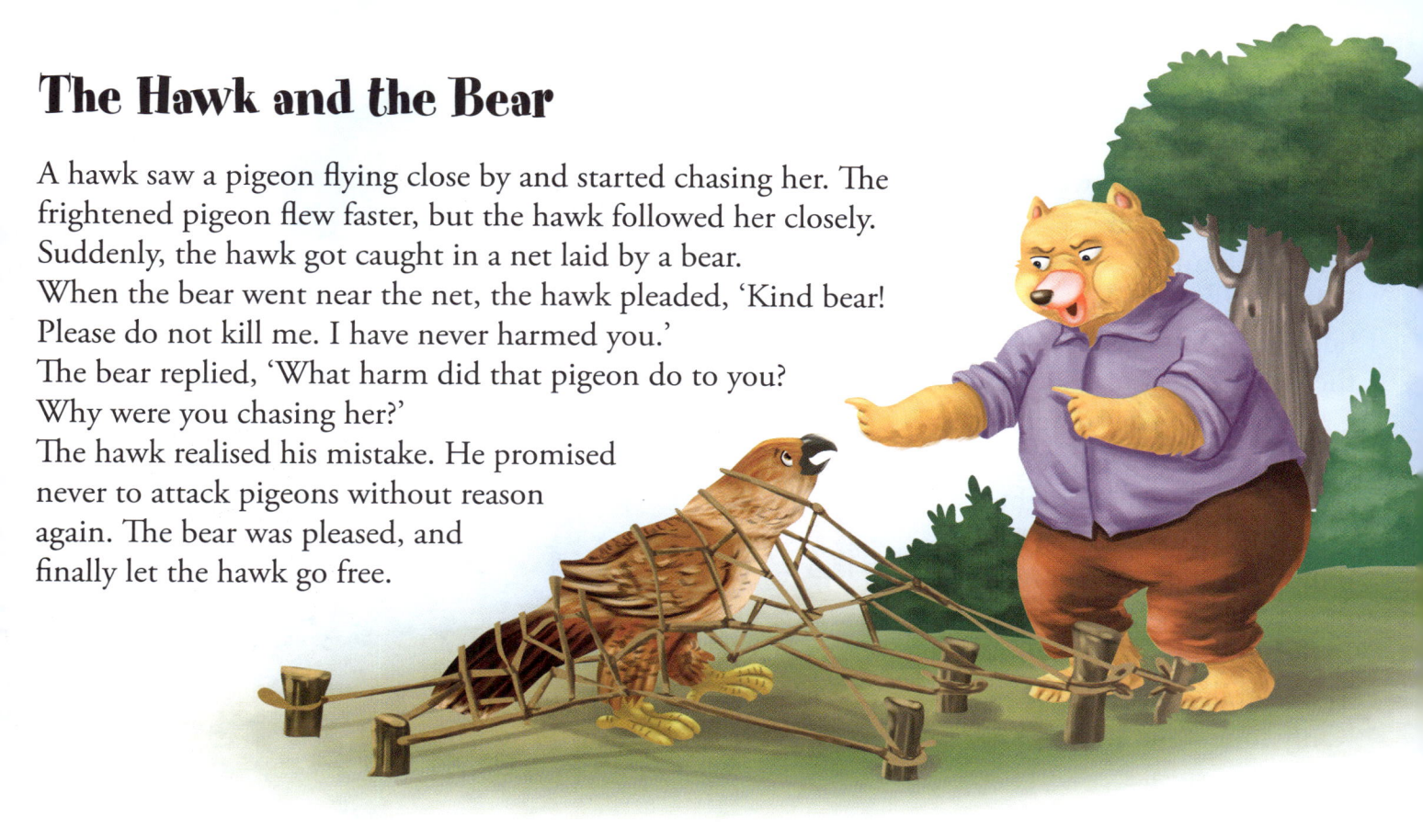

A hawk saw a pigeon flying close by and started chasing her. The frightened pigeon flew faster, but the hawk followed her closely. Suddenly, the hawk got caught in a net laid by a bear.
When the bear went near the net, the hawk pleaded, 'Kind bear! Please do not kill me. I have never harmed you.'
The bear replied, 'What harm did that pigeon do to you? Why were you chasing her?'
The hawk realised his mistake. He promised never to attack pigeons without reason again. The bear was pleased, and finally let the hawk go free.

The Poor Pigeon

A crow and a pigeon were friends. One day, they were flying over a village.
They saw a cow-herd, with a pot of curd on his head, walking ahead of them. The wicked crow went after the man and put his beak into the pot to eat the curd.
When the cow-herd saw this, he tried to catch the crow. But the crow flew away.
However, the cow-herd hit the pigeon with a stone and hurt it. The poor pigeon wailed, 'Just because my friend behaved badly, I had to suffer!'
He was never friends with the wicked crow again.

The Lion and the Fox

A hungry lion once went into a fox's cave. He thought, 'I will hide here and eat the fox when he returns.'
When the fox reached his cave, he saw the lion's footprints going in. He understood the lion's plan at once, and said, 'Hello Cave, why are you so quiet today?'
The lion thought that the cave actually spoke. He thought that it must be quiet because he was hiding there. He did not want the fox to suspect anything, so he said, 'Please come in.'
The fox ran away, saying, 'Only fools would believe that a cave speaks!'

The Sly Lion

A lion, a wolf, a jackal and a sheep were friends and promised to share their food.
One day, the wolf caught a stag. The lion divided it into four parts.
The lion took the best piece, saying, 'This is mine.'
He took another portion, saying, 'This is for being the bravest.'
The lion then took the third piece, and said, 'That's for being the biggest.'
Then, he said with a loud roar, 'Whoever wants the last portion should fight me for it.'
The other three went away, saying, 'We cannot be friends with such a sly and unfair fellow!'

What Ringo Learnt

Ringo was a bear cub who lived in a forest. Ringo's mother taught him, 'Son, you must always be alert, even when drinking from the river.'

She taught him about the seasons, and how to catch the fish from the river without falling in.

Many years passed, and Ringo's mother died. But he always remembered what she had taught him.

One day Ringo thought, 'Mother taught me to fish and to be smart, alert and patient. I should teach these lessons to other animals as well.'

From that day, Ringo became the teacher for all the animals in the forest!

The Heron, the Snake and the Mongoose

A family of herons lived on a tree. Near the tree, there lived a black snake, which often troubled the birds.

A wicked crab lived nearby. He wanted to eat the herons. So he thought of a plan.

The crab advised the herons to steal meat from the mongoose and throw it into the snake's hole. The herons did what the crab said. Sure enough, the mongoose killed the snake.

The crab climbed up the tree and said, 'Now that the snake is not guarding the tree, I can come up and eat you!'

And that is what he did.

White-Paw and the Kind Hawk

White-Paw, a wolf cub, lived with his mother. One evening, while chasing a butterfly, White-Paw wandered deep into the forest. There, some cruel hyenas carried him to their camp. They said, 'This wolf cub shall be our servant.'

They made him work all day and gave him very little to eat. The cub was miserable.

A hawk saw the cub working hard. He felt sorry for the little fellow, and rescued White-Paw. He dropped the cub near his house.

White-Paw and his mother were very happy to see each other. They both thanked the kind hawk for his help.

The Elephant and the Giraffe

A giraffe took her cattle to graze in a field. The elephant also brought his sheep there. But one of the giraffe's bulls killed one of the sheep.

The elephant said, 'My bull has killed your sheep.'

The giraffe knew this was not possible, but said, 'You should give me your sheep in return.'

The elephant answered, 'Actually, it was your bull that killed my sheep.'

The giraffe angrily said, 'I will not pay you.'

The elephant said, 'You must be willing to do what you want others to do!'

The giraffe was ashamed and quietly paid the elephant for the sheep that had been killed.

Tina, the Kind Doe

Tina, the doe, was very rich and kind. All the animals loved her. This made the other deer very jealous.

One day, a few deer told Tina, 'We have offered our riches to the river-goddess so that she will bless us.'

Tina thought this was a very good idea. She ran home and brought all her valuables. But as soon as she threw them into the river, the deer who were jealous of Tina started laughing.

They said, 'We fooled you! Now we have riches and you don't!'

Suddenly, the river-goddess appeared. She blessed Tina, returned her valuables and punished the other deer for their jealousy.

Elsie's Precious Jewels

A lioness named Elsie went with her two cubs to visit a friend.

Elsie's friend was very grandly dressed, with many jewels. She gave the cubs many nice things to eat.

'Mother's friend is so beautiful,' said one cub.

'She is not as beautiful as our mother,' argued the other.

In the meantime, Elsie's friend noticed that she was dressed very simply and said, 'My dear Elsie, are you very poor now?'

Elsie hugged her cubs and smiled. 'No,' she said, 'I am not poor. My sons are my gems and are more precious than all your jewels!'

The Fox Cub

A lion once found a fox cub in the forest. He said to the lioness, 'Let us raise him along with our two cubs.'
The three cubs grew up as brothers. Some months later, they saw an elephant. The lion cubs faced him bravely, but the fox cub ran away.
The lioness said to the fox cub, 'Don't be ashamed. You are a fox and foxes don't attack elephants. But my sons may attack you when they realise you are not a lion. It is time for you to live with foxes.'
Thus, the fox cub left the lion's family.

The Lion and his Brothers

A lion had been travelling for many months. When he returned home, he was happy because his brothers had organised a feast. He exclaimed, 'I am lucky to have such loving brothers!'
But his brothers were secretly jealous of him. They planned to kill him by adding poison to his food.
One of the lion's friend overheard the brothers' plan. Thus, before the lion could eat, he knocked the lion's food away.
A cat ran up to eat the fallen food, and fainted at once. The lion's brothers were so afraid of being punished, that they ran away and never came back.